The Cosmos of Soul

A Wake-up Call for Humanity

Patricia Cori

Gateway

Gateway
an imprint of
Gill & Macmillan Ltd
Hume Avenue
Park West
Dublin 12
with associated companies throughout the world
www.gillmacmillan.ie

© 2000 Patricia Jo Cori

0 7171 3056 8

Index compiled by Alick Bartholomew
Print origination by Carole Lynch
Illustrations by Alanna Corballis
Printed in Malaysia

A catalogue record is available for this book
from the British Library.

3 5 4

To my mother, Sara,
For teaching me to reach
for the Dream
and...

to Franco
for sharing
It
with me.

CONTENTS

FOREWORD

It is an unprecedented moment — this entering into the new millennium — and so much is available to us now that has been held secret over the centuries. We have arrived. We are at the doorway, about to turn the key and walk through.

Extraordinary things are happening with great rapidity now, at the beginning of the Golden Age of Humanity, and we are priv-il-eged — the New Aquarians. Mysteries regarding humankind's true history are coming to light and it seems we are rediscovering our-selves, developing our potential as future pioneers of new worlds in space. And although the exciting new breakthroughs in science and archaeology are generally easier to embrace than those of the metaphysical realm, it does not mean they are necessarily more significant — nor are they separate, as we are discovering. Nonetheless, claims of channelled voices from the 'sixth dimension' do test even the most open-minded; so why would I want to subject myself to the inevitable criticism and ridicule that could quite possibly result from declaring this book authored by 'extraterrestrials' from the beyond?

Don't think I haven't asked myself that question many times over the past year, as I watched these teachings take form in the written word. In the end, I trust the integrity of the work and the intention behind it. I also believe that the content of this material will reach others as truth that they already know within them-selves, bringing hope and empowerment to those who read these pages. In addition, I keep asking myself, why is it any more diffi-cult to believe that a human being can pick up and record thought waves than it is to accept that a transistor radio can pick up and broadcast radio waves?

After the initial shock, curiosity and scepticism of my first experience transcribing messages from the Speakers of the Sirian

Council, I realised that there is nothing more to this than simply tuning in to another frequency — another station, so to speak. For whatever reason, it seems that my antennae are picking up a thought band of cosmic transmissions that comes into my mind like radio waves to a stereo. In the end, it is a simple and natural process. Animals also tune in; they just don't have our capacity to communicate their perceptions verbally. We, the human race, are capable of receiving and transmitting thoughts on many levels and we have the ability to transform those impulses into words. We can reach each other on different frequency bands, just as we can and do communicate with beings on other planes of consciousness. All too often, we forget just how truly remarkable we are!

My work with the Speakers has always taken place in the predawn hours, when interference from fields of traversing electromagnetic waves is at its lowest ebb and the channels are the most clear. This, I have been told, is the 'violet hour' of Gaia; and so since the early days of transcribing *The Cosmos of Soul* I had to adjust my life for the early morning galactic alarm clock: a sound not unlike the tuning in of a radio station. Soon after the static interference in my sleep, the messages would begin. Nudged from my deepest dream states, I would crawl into the kitchen, turn on the coffee, head for the computer room and watch the keyboard spring to life with the words you are about to read.

The coffee pot still burns overtime and other projects have been forgotten, since the Speakers continue to broadcast their message. A second book, *The Dark Side of Atlantis*, is emerging from the process. I still long for a full night of uninterrupted sleep, but I am just as mystified and excited today as I was the very first time I made contact and I am 'eternally' grateful to be part of the process that brings these teachings — their teachings — to the world.

In truth, I have been consciously communicating with spirit beings as far back in my childhood as I can remember, but only recently did I make the connection. Many times as a child I found myself surrounded by strange, twinkling lights that would nest in the leaves of the trees of our garden — clearly the kind of thing a kid doesn't talk about. My mother says she used to wonder how I could entertain myself for so many hours by myself. Little did she know that with me was a cast of loving spirit guides who were teaching me through play. Little did I know that these were to be only the beginnings of contact with extradimensional beings who would be guiding my course for many years to come.

It has been a wondrous journey, serving and learning from such brilliant guides, multidimensional beings of great compassion and wisdom. Their message is a 'wake up call' for humanity, delivered to those of us who dare to step out of the mould of convention. It is for those who question and seek, feeling our way from the heart — reclaiming the power and the light.

If you are sceptical, as was I, of channelled transmissions from other worlds and dimensions, remember: what is important here is the message, not the messenger. Let yourself believe in possibilities, however remote and far-reaching. Try on new ideas and express your freedom. In challenging your convictions, you widen your horizons and open the doors of your mind.

Many are the voices now guiding us through the portals, as we plunge deep into our memory of the future.

Patricia Cori
Scribe for the Speakers of the Sirian High Council

May, 2000

One

'LET THERE BE LIGHT...'

'... And God said, "Let there be light." And there was light.'

Know that without the darkness there could have been no contrast, no point of reference in such a godly pronouncement, and understand how the Creator is just as omnisciently Lord of the Sacred Darkness as of the Blessed Light.

In this difficult time of transition, as human consciousness is being blasted out to both extremes of the poles, chaos has manifested as a constant in your world. Yet, within its fibre, its whirling frenzy, is laced the order underlying all life and intelligence in the Cosmos. There is order in chaos, however veiled in the subtle mysteries of nature's illusive rhythms. Once you understand and incorporate this truth into your awareness, you will flow in the wake of change just as falling leaves dance and pirouette in the wind.

Technology is delivering information from every corner of your planet with such rapidity that it is short-circuiting the neurological networks of your minds. It is too much, too fast. You are being distracted from the universal picture and programmed to perceive your master, technology, as the Great Liberator. Haven't

you realised yet that you are becoming enslaved by your computers and the techno-grid of the 'Net'? The information industry
has moved far ahead of your ability to conceive of its potential
impact upon the future of all life forms on Gaia, while you are
being spoon-fed only what it feels you will be able to first absorb
and then purchase. Recognise, however, that every new electronic
instrument is already obsolete well before the cashiers ring up their
hi-tech invoices and Wall Street grooms you for the next level.

Information regarding the government's secret alliance with
alien intelligence is being methodically leaked to you in the same
way, because you are deemed emotionally incapable of dealing
with extraplanetary life and the implications of alien intervention
on Earth. But you do understand ... for you are **starseed**.

So many of you are now reclaiming your stellar wisdom that
the governments and the hierarchy from whom they receive their
mandates simply cannot keep the truth from you any longer. You
have moved beyond searching for clues or tangible proof and are
reconnecting with galactic intelligence. There are those of you
who have adjusted your frequencies to serve as direct channels
for transmissions from other dimensions, and this is now moving
from the shadow of ridicule and distrust into the mainstream consciousness of lightworkers across the planet. You are plugging
back into the Akasha — wisdom you access throughout existence
— and it is that knowing at the very deepest level of your being
that we shall refer to as '**centre**'.

Let us begin with birth. Your God-consciousness has been so
distorted by male-dominated religions that many of you would
believe your very birth a 'sin'. You have been taught that you are
guilty from birth of the shame and sin of sexual union between
your parents, who still carry the guilt and shame of the proverbial
eating of the apple in Eden — the original sin. Do you think about
the absurdity of original sin and how religious empires have been
formed around your belief in it? Baptism, whereby you are cleansed
of the impurity of that sin, is representative of those rituals designed
to programme you into believing not only that God lies outside
you ... but that by kneeling before the administrators of the

judgmental God, you may just receive the absolution necessary to squeak through your earthly lives and find your way into heaven.

We ask you to question the hypocrisy of any religion that would sanction and encourage sexual union for the express purpose of bearing children, while any other sexual expression is totally forbidden, even in the so-called sanctity of marriage. Despite the blessing of the marital union, the child must still undergo baptism to cleanse it of the sin of creation.

Haven't you had enough of such religious manipulation to question its true intention? How can birth — the deliverance of life through the sacred darkness of the womb — possibly be tainted or impure? Why must the Goddess Mother be virginal, when the miracle of new life — the ultimate manifestation of the God-light — is sparked through the explosive union of woman with man? By asking yourselves how and why you have allowed these alienating religious canons to separate you from the very process of God's emergence between you, you begin the process of letting go and 'letting God' **within** you. Indeed, many of you are now releasing yourselves from the holds of the dogma, recognising your godliness, and we commend you for your courage and your vision.

You are becoming empowered now with an expanding awareness of how your souls twinkle in the night skies of your being like the stars in the heavens, and how glorious is your birth into physical reality. Many of you have understood, while others are still floundering — lost in the confusion of the power systems of church and religion, governments and societies which build upon your feelings of shame, guilt and alienation from Prime Creator, *The All-That-Is, That-Has-Ever-Been and That-Always-Will-Be*. You have yet to imagine what immense power lies in your mastery of human sexuality, for they have cleverly disempowered you with fig leaves and ignoble allegory. That archetypal memory of forbidden fruit and disobedience has been deliberately stimulated within you throughout many civilisations subject to their controlling influence.

You are sparks from the flame, fragments of the Absolute, choosing to exercise free will in your descent into matter again and again — gods in your own right. As conscious beings, you experience and learn the alchemy of transcending matter and returning to spirit, the true purpose of the ascent along the evolutionary spiral towards illumination. However long the journey home, as co-creators you are joining together to return to Source in the perpetual cycle of life.

Imagine, just as the shimmerings of fiery brilliance exploding out as radiance of your Solar Deity and slowly cooling, take form as celestial bodies in your solar system, so does all consciousness break from the light and in descending into physical reality take on the 'crust' or outer shell of the physical body. As the God-consciousness of Gaia reaches out from her fiery core, permeating every layer of her body and etheric shield — the ozone — so do you. Through this metaphor of life/spirit awareness, we ask you to come now to clarity regarding the question of living from the centre of your being.

You can find your way through the maze of outer reality and the illusions of appearance by returning to centre, that perfect oneness of dark and light within all things. It is the yin/yang balance, the nurturing cool of magnetism which cradles the spark of your electrifying radiance. It is here that the soul is seated, and from here and here alone will you find the truth to guide you through your storms. Like a lighthouse, it is the beacon of all your experience as you ride the waves of Earth's tumultuous journey upward along the evolutionary coil. Until you return to that centre place — the seat of the soul — you will feel powerless and afraid in the wake of the great transformation that has begun on Earth.

From a position of balance and acceptance you will recognise creation in chaos, the emergence of light from darkness once again repeating itself in the theatre of life. Rather than fearfully trembling on your knees you will cluster together in breathtaking patterns of brilliantly coloured spectra: the Gossamer Web of Light. Together with your galactic family, you will experience firsthand the absolute perfection of creation unfolding — the divine explosion — a radiance that you, as incarnate souls, will have the privilege to choose to experience bodily very soon in the future.

Put away your images of the apocalyptic final curtain. They do not serve you, and will only fuel the fears of annihilation which keep you swinging further and further outwards on the emotional pendulum. You must be at centre, in balance, if you are to correctly run the energy through your body circuitry. At the hub of the spinning wheel, you will feel only minimally the centrifugal force of Gaia's revolution.

Understandably, as you pass now across the great divide of your linear time-frame — the new millennium — humankind is experiencing a vibrational surge of great intensity. The force of such energy rolling through you will make you feel, at times, like you are absolutely losing touch with yourselves — and in a positive sense you are doing exactly that, while moving beyond the sensate experience and the confines of three-dimensional awareness. You are to shed your skins, as it were, and leave them behind; because you are being reborn into the fifth Earth race of Aquarian men and women.

The anaesthesia is wearing off and the human race is being forced to experience and feel what is happening to Gaia and her children. You had become so numbed by the scenes of brutality, destruction and darkness; so exasperated by media exploitation, that the Power had to turn up the frequency in order to reach you. If, after all, you are so drugged that you cannot feel fear and despair then you cannot be manipulated to react in mass mind, and we suggest that you consider this scenario as one true cause of suffering in the world. You are marketed and brainwashed to it.

Once you have been programmed to believe that God is outside you and that you are sinners from birth, you are spiritually owned by the dogma. From there, manipulating you into mass behavioural modes which serve the power élite is child's play to the Authority. One example is the war drama being perpetrated time and time again by your governments.

Today it is Yugoslavia and the New World Order which play dramatically upon your peace of mind. The scenes are intensifying, but the story-line of war and destruction generally follows a recurring theme. Not so long ago you were inflamed by the first images of another war, the Bosnian conflict, as domestic unrest there developed into global front page news. Do you even remember? What was the catalyst of separation and rage that transformed peaceful men into murderous animals, maiming their brothers, slaughtering the children ... leaving helpless women raped and forever defeated? Did you, conscious human beings, ever really understand the seed of that conflagration? What covert mechanics were at work there in Bosnia, inciting the cold hatred and darkest emotion among beings who had previously managed to live in peaceful coexistence?

As the situation escalated, indignant government leaders of your United Nations World Government carefully sidestepped intervention, while they positioned themselves against the horrors of war and violence, and yet some of those very nations were capitalising on the escalation, selling arms and war machinery to either or both sides. All the while, you were reassured with images of your leaders 'seeking a peaceful solution' and many talks — so many talks of peace. Under the table, arms traded fast and furiously, and your world watched in impotence and despair the travesty of the human condition. You may remember your initial horror as scenes of mutilation and death were broadcast, and within a very short time you sat mindlessly carving into your steaks, while gazing into the blood of the innocent stained across your screens.

Now, as your attention is once again focused in the Balkan territories, the Warriors of World Order have intervened with bigger and better arms of destruction than those they sold to the 'little brother'. While humanity fears that escalation of the conflict might lead to nuclear winter, rest assured that that is not the intention of the Secret Government,[1] the hierarchy of power on Planet Earth. Rather, they are using the theatre of war to test much more sophisticated tools of destruction involving mass mood manipulation and communications control systems. The bombs are mere camouflage and distraction.

The plot is intensifying now and the danger is immense, yet so many human beings still choose to bury their heads in the sands of ego-centred isolation, hoping the chilling winds of man's unkindness will blow past them and away. Hoping that all will be resolved and that soon this, too, will be only last year's forgotten news. Hoping that the pain and suffering will never reach their shores or touch their personal lives.

Because you are so bombarded with images of devastation, you become easily anaesthetised and have learned to shut down your pain sensors in order to cope with it all. That indifference is the true reason the intensity of human violence and despair has reached such an unbearable level. You were not reacting anymore and so they turned up the frequency, for without your fear and hopelessness they have no power over you. This they understand all too well. It is the reason they continuously stimulate your worry and dismay over the possible unhappy ending: the 'final curtain', a no-way-out story-line of total and complete annihilation.

Considering that your food supply is poisoned, Gaia's rich forests are disappearing and her oceans are dying, it is difficult to see your way back to harmony. Many of you are out somewhere hanging from a cliff, clutching your emotional lifelines — your fear, guilt and powerlessness — waiting for the fall. However, what more and more of you are now experiencing is the trans-mutation of chaos into order, once again ... as in the beginning. Just as from the darkness of the womb did your mother writhe and shake in the pain of your passage through the birth canal, so now the Earth Mother is shuddering in the darkness of the night, as she prepares for her rebirth into the brilliance of the light and her ascent upon the spiral of evolution.

Note
1. See chapter 11.

Two

EMANCIPATION

It is time to liberate yourselves, if you are to achieve what you came here to accomplish as members of the dawning. The process of liberation begins with the simple desire to recognise the bondage of any axiom, paradigm or structure which stirs within you feelings of impotence and resignation. Once the jailer has been identified, you can lift off the chains that have bound you to those belief structures just as effortlessly as you have placed them around your necks.

Know that your televisions serve you best when they are unplugged, for your precious minds are beginning to know the quickening that is occurring in Planet Earth's vibrational fields and you would be wise to remove the conditioning instruments that interfere with that process. Test yourselves, remembering that if you cannot do without, then you are addicted. You may also wish to silence your computers and any extraneous noise and distractions for a limited time within the home environment, so that you may experience your thoughts and emotions without the numbing sounds and images being blasted out at rates your conscious minds cannot even perceive. We urge you to unplug your dishwashers, remote telephones, microwaves and similar devices; allowing your precious natural body rhythms to realign, freed from the electromagnetic radiation emissions that are tearing and depleting your protective shields — your auras — just as these pollutants are contributing to the destruction of the ozone of your planet.

If you are still uninformed about the health hazards of electromagnetic emissions being beamed at you from every direction (inside and outside your homes, workplaces and city streets), learn now what steps can be taken to minimise the negative effects they are having on your mental, emotional and physical bodies. Monumental consumption and wasteful use of energy creates this — one of the most insidious forms of pollution resulting on the blue-green planet.

Electromagnetic radiation alters the subtle energy fields around your bodies, effectively short-circuiting you, yet most of you have very limited awareness of how long-term exposure will affect your thoughts, emotions and physical states of health. Your homes are filling more and more with many unnecessary electrical gadgets (all emitters at some level), but the greatest offenders are televisions, computers, satellite dishes, remote telephones and microwave ovens. Every time a current passes down a wire it is radiated out into the environment, penetrating Earth's auric field and emanating out into space, just as vast quantities are absorbed into your many-layered fields as beings 'in body'. Entrained as you are by your appliances such as computers, stereo equipment and electric lighting, you have turned yourselves into human guinea pigs, living in the killing fields of traversing electrical frequencies, accumulating radiation even when you sleep. The body's natural energy meridians are eventually thrown off and altered, resulting in illness and emotional imbalance.

Microwave ovens are particularly devastating. Despite the safety guarantees provided in sales propaganda, they emanate dangerously high levels of electromagnetic radiation. Long-term exposure can result in acute states of disharmony within the physical body, such as infertility and cancer. They are, in fact, a primary reason why these two particular diseases are increasing at such alarming rates in your westernised cultures. Their emanations are also reaching out into the Cosmos, creating disturbance on other planes. You are polluting the galaxy — interfering with the environments of other worlds — and this is simply **not acceptable**.

We ask why you believe you cannot live without this deadly microwave oven. As if it were not enough that it is belching electro-magnetic radiation emissions into your homes, the environment and beyond; it works by rearranging the molecular structure of your food. In simplistic terms, these molecules slam into each other, the friction creates heat and the food is instantaneously cooked.

Here is another concern you may not have yet duly considered — one which we advise you to place in the foreground of your conscious thoughts regarding health and the environment — with particular focus on the widespread use of microwave cooking. Do you understand what happens when chemicals and hormones utilised to process and preserve food undergo molecular alteration? Greater than the loss of any nutritional value in the food is the toxicity of additives, chemicals, and hormones that are destabilising in the process of molecular alteration. You have not even begun to imagine the long-term effects this will have on your physical and subtle bodies.

Unstable chemicals in dead food. Is this what you intend as feeding and nourishing the body? You rationalise that microwave ovens are a great time-saver. We ask, 'What is your hurry?' Do you ever question it? In truth, you are subliminally sold to believe that there is not enough time in order to keep you buying the latest time-saver technologies, with which you ironically believe to be working in 'real time'. Consider, too, that by seducing yourselves into zapping food (your sustenance) in microwaves to save time (so that you have more time to gaze long hours into your video devices), you are again serving the Power and denying yourselves the richness of simply being in the 'now' experience of your earthly lives. You are rendering yourselves passive targets, distracted again from the bigger picture.

There is something quite unreal about 'real time' in such a context. Until you understand that there is only **the moment**, and that all else is illusion, you will never develop that sense of serenity and self-awareness that comes with being at centre, at one with your surroundings — living the absolute experience of your 'now' moment, masters of your mind, body and emotions.

And so, we do encourage you to reject in their entirety these microwave devices and develop a new approach to preparing and eating healthy, life-enhancing food which breaks down in the exquisite process of metabolism and becomes who you are. You have all the time you need without them. Embrace the art of cooking as an expression of your love, imagination and artistry. You will notice the difference in the taste and quality of what you eat; you will be sending the message of love into your beings; and your homes will be filled with aromas, rather than radiation.

Recently, industry has begun irradiating fruits and vegetables, which helps them maintain their fresh appearance for a longer shelf-life in your stores and markets. They, too, are nutritionally dead. The live enzymes and all nutrients in the food are destroyed, but those beautiful looking strawberries hold their brilliant red patina so much longer. The strategy is to kill the enzymatic process (the live elements) that leads to ripening which, in turn, reduces spoiling. You keep buying longer and voilà — profits increase!

Clearly, the harmful effects of irradiated foods on public health are hardly a primary concern of the perpetrators of such technology; nor of the regulating bodies of your governments who are allowing it. No, it appears you are simply going to have to look after your own health and nutrition from now on. We suggest you consider these points carefully whenever you trustingly wheel your grocery trolleys down the aisles of your favourite supermarkets, admiring the freshness of the fruits and vegetables there and believing that, by choosing the biggest and brightest produce, you are doing what is best for your bodies.

Isn't it enough that you are being blasted with electromagnetic radiation from the environment? Surely you don't wish to be processing radiation-treated foods through your digestive tracts, and into your blood and lymphatic systems as well! Together with others in your communities, you can boycott irradiated foods and refuse to ingest these toxins, and you will see that the phenomenon will disappear. It is simply a matter of how far you will allow yourselves to be pushed and how loud your collective voice will sound out against manipulation of your well-being. Will you hand your well-being over to profit-seeking industries and the corrupt governmental agencies which serve them, or will you join together to become a united front, one body, a conscious society? You can direct the outcome of this reality by becoming aware of the poisonous effects of irradiation in your foods and then bringing the message to your communities. Become an activist; write to consumer organisations and the media; talk to store managers; gather with like-minded individuals in your areas to boycott all such food products on your shelves. They will disappear when you stop buying them — plain and simple.

Of foods that are harmful to you we suggest you give due consideration to the toxins in meat and meat products, and we do note that more and more of you are simply losing your taste for animal flesh. Here, too, industry has exacerbated the negative effects of ingesting meat, now treated with growth hormones, pesticides, antibiotics and other poisons utilised to increase production and sell more to make more. Fortunately, growing numbers of you simply will not be able to eat meat much longer, and you will find it is effortless to let it go. It is keeping you glued down in density at a time when you are initiating the process of transmutation into light body.

We can tell you that the syndrome you have named the 'mad cow disease' has been created on astral levels by higher beings who are instructing and guiding you in this aspect of your conscious awakening, for it is essential now that you understand the importance of ingesting life rather than death. Your safe passage depends on it.

Before the Sirian keys can be activated, you must clear your fields and release as much as possible of the accumulation of poisons and disturbances from your mental, emotional and physical bodies; so that your receptive capacities are enhanced enough to handle the overwhelming levels of energy which will be passing through you. We are telling you, in your terms, that as Gaia enters the next vibrational phase of her evolution, you will either light up like Christmas trees or blow your fuses — like an entire Manhattan city block gone dark from a spark. If you can feel and internalise the analogy of Earth as the macrocosm of your individual mental-emotional-physical bodies, you will understand what is happening to you as three-dimensional beings and how the Earth Changes are a reflection of the process that has begun its most significant phase of alteration.

Gaia's primary disease is rooted in the excessive overpopulation. Like cancer, the population rate is increasing at astronomical speed, killing off the other healthy cells ... the sentient beings and life forms attempting to share what remains of the garden. Species are rapidly becoming extinct, the once lush forests levelled, the waters poisoned, and as this cancer grows it suffocates the life out of the body of Gaia by consuming everything in its path. Yet, nature as divine consciousness does indeed adjust itself, and you are now experiencing the phenomenon of a sudden dramatic drop in the sperm count of the male species in all corners of the planet. It is nature's way of correcting the imbalance.

Too many beings requiring water, food and space are consuming too much of Gaia's resources, creating devastating waste and shortages. Why do you think the AIDS virus was created? A less violent virus was genetically restructured in a laboratory, and the diabolical idea that the antidote was simultaneously manufactured is in truth a reality, although by mutation the cure became invalid. As with most viruses, the mutated strains are more deadly, more devastating, and are resistant to the primary antidote — so now the virus is completely out of control. The AIDS virus and others now being prepared in your underground laboratories are simply population control technologies designed to re-establish equilibrium in the body count on the planet.

If you can see beyond the horror of such widespread genocide, you may understand the bigger issue here. As man has altered the balance and the population has run amok, some huge catastrophe has had to occur to reduce your numbers dramatically, and this the governments of the world understand. As medicine, living conditions and food sources have raised the lifespan considerably (while birth control is still forbidden by most religions and unknown in many third world countries), you have the unthinkable scenario of six billion human beings exploding into twenty within a twenty-year time-frame. The Mother cannot sustain the load she carries now, much less a tripling, and this is reflected in her belching and violent rebellion as the earthquakes, volcanoes and crashing seas reflect. She is shaking you off, like a bridled stallion rebelling against the weight of the would-be master.

Uncontrolled growth consumes everything in its path, another reason why the governments of Earth create wars, biological weaponry and famines. Death is essential to life. This is the paradox that seems to elude humanity. You cling to your physical reality because you have yet to understand your immortality and, cloaked in your ignorance, your noble intention to save human life at all costs, you are killing the animals, streams and riches of Gaia's biological pool. You are sucking out her rich oil, ripping apart her mineral core and choking her with your waste. This in the name of respect for life.

At a time when Earth's population was in harmony with the rest of the planet, the rivers flowed clear and brilliant, luxuriant gardens filled your lungs with oxygen, and humankind flourished. But it is man who has destroyed the balance and warned, continues ruthlessly to rape Gaia and so, unless you unite and move rapidly to save her — to raise the vibration — it shall be Gaia herself and only she who will rectify the disharmony.

You may rest easier knowing that in the perfection of the All-That-Is and the eternal progression of existence, all things eventually resolve for the highest purpose. Still, each microcosmic unit is involved in the playing out of the process.

You have **choice**. You accept responsibility for the unfolding of your lives. You create your own realities, affecting with every breath that of the Whole.

This is the power of knowing the God within you.

Three

CONSCIOUS CLEARING

Much information is available regarding the work that must be undertaken to clear your bodies of the illnesses, toxins, negative thought forms and energy blocks that you carry within you. You have but to set your intention and the process is initiated.

It is a time of returning to the holistic method, tuning into the layers of consciousness and toning the entire being — from the higher astral down into the physical — and you are fortunate to have many trained lightworkers in body now, serving as catalysts. There are also many false healers who would take your power from you, feeding upon you like parasites upon the host. Remember in selecting the facilitator that it is you who are the true healers and your intent, the focused will, that sets things in motion. In your desperate search for the light, be cautious of the new-found saviours and modern Messiahs. There are many who, recognising your need, have greatly profited from these archetypes and many more are preening, for here there is much to be gained and the ego of the unawakened never rests. Many charlatans have donned the robes of the White Brotherhood. They are masters of metaphysical rhetoric, and will try to mesmerise and persuade you with utterances of quite complex and abstract realities. Many are the dark warriors, albeit the disguises, so be discerning, for the stakes are higher than ever.

To recognise genuine lightworkers, ponder these simple questions: do they empower you to heal yourselves or would they have you follow their doctrines and worship at their temples? Do they encourage your self-discovery and awareness, directing you inward, or are they pointing 'the way', pushing you down their path of 'illumination'? Do they honour your power, or take it from you?

True healing is a simple, loving ability to channel the light —
a gift of those who love unconditionally and who have chosen to
serve others as they, too, become beacons of the heart. The light
does not initiate with them, for they merely serve as vehicles of
Spirit. Anyone who would have you believe otherwise, and there
are many, is operating from ego-centred consciousness and not
from love. Do not be fooled by the paraphernalia, guises and
rituals of their white robes and altars; rather, establish contact
through the eyes (windows of the soul), where you will be able
to uncover true meaning and intention behind any façade. You
will have to look deep within the eyes of the other, searching for
the soul light ... deeper than ever before.

Those light ones who have come to assist in this transition wish
to empower you to finding your own truth. They will not accept
your glorifying of their knowledge, or fanning their egos, and will
refuse your worship. Servants of the light, they have come to help
you back to centre, as you learn to trust your intuition and turn up
your flame. By opening the channel and allowing the light to flow
through, they are serving as the third in the triangulation process
of Spirit. As the light passes through them it is further directed into
the darker corners of your beings, those places where you hold
trapped pain and memories which you are now ready to examine
and release — in the light of your rising awareness. When you are
ready, and only then, will the healing occur. You alone set the
stage for this awakening, for you are the magicians and no one
else possesses the power unless you give yours away.

It is an important lesson, that of confronting the ego. You
struggle all your lives to nourish it, the wounding beginning in
early childhood when you are too young to understand the
essence of pain. As you learn to identify and fortify yourselves as
individuals, you are confronted with conditioned experiences of
the immediate environment and the people who form the core of
your emotional lives. In the confusion of establishing the Self, you
are at once taught to be selfless and obeying and at the same time
to stand up for yourselves: to speak, then to be silent; to walk and
to then stay put; to play, and to behave. It is a long journey, the

learning road, for you must undo so many erroneous perceptions that have taken seed within you and release your egos completely, in total self-recognition — accepting that there is only the whole, the One ... no separation. It is a process that requires much introspection, forgiveness and vision.

Many superb teachers are here to guide you and more are coming through to Earth on the next wave. During this phase of your transformation, great numbers of individuals are being cleared as messengers of stellar consciousness, and vast amounts of information are being made available to facilitate your ascension into the higher frequencies as you prepare for full immersion. Your true spirit leaders are those who are teaching you to honour self and the Earth; your brother and your enemy; and all sentient beings. Through their humility and love-centred consciousness, they reflect the light of Supreme Being — the All-That-Is — to help guide you home.

More and more of you are spreading the light of love as you gather the beams around and throughout your world, building and enhancing the Gossamer Web. You have been told of the great grid that was thrown around your planet by the controlling forces of the Annunaki[1] at a time when they believed they would own you forever by stripping you of your resources. We ask that you begin to visualise the golden web that your love is spinning through that grid: triangular light forms folding out and interconnecting with the light ones of the furthest reaches of the galaxy. It will be the undoing of the grid, now at the point of disintegration, as the control experiment simply did not work and the Annunaki (ancestral warriors of the galaxy) are dying in the cold darkness of their hunger.

The cleansing and clearing of your etheric bodies has begun, and there is much light emanating from Gaia out into the Cosmos, drawing beings from every dimension to your world at this time of shifting. We ask that in healing the fragments and crises within, you also become aware of every other living thing and send out love and acceptance — for until you learn the interconnectedness of all life you will never truly be healed.

You will be most effective when you have gazed into the soul mirrors of another and seen your own existence, your fire, reflected back. It will not be enough to clear your fields and heal the pain if you remain insular. You are interconnected, and only by drawing the others up into the light along with you will the greater purpose be served.

Gaia prepares for her emergence. This is your mission, regardless of the disguises life has donned as you play out the scenes.

We are calling upon you to integrate.

Note

1. Annunaki: Ancestral warriors from Niburu, a remote planet whose elliptical orbit around the Sun completes a cycle every 3,600 Earth years.

   Suggested reading: Sitchin, Zechariah, *When Time Began*, Avon Books.

Four

OPENING THE ARCHIVES

You are still searching for the Great Halls of Learning in a three-dimensional context, which is partially the reason you have not yet uncovered the chamber buried within the Earth Sphinx. You hope to open a magical door which would unfold a gilded library containing all the secrets of creation — the curtain lifts and humanity receives the teachings: the answers to the unknown. Know that this picture is quite distant from the reality that awaits you at the revealing of the symbolic halls, which you believe lie hidden in the sands under the Great Sphinx at Giza.

Although you are learning genetics and the DNA matrix, and have begun to decode the Secret Wisdom embedded there, the enigma of its immensity has escaped you … so hear it again now — the cosmic library lies coded within your DNA.

> As Above, So Below.
> The blueprint of the macrocosm
> is buried within the microcosm
> and all is infinite.
> From the seed the unfolding and from the tree
> regeneration.

Consider that your genetic science gods, having only just scraped the surface, have reproduced life from a blueprint. You have been teased with Dolly, the cloned ewe, but rest assured that far more intricate works of genetic manipulation are underway and, as in Atlantis, many terrifying mutations and mutilations have resulted. You have pondered the potential horror of such capabilities in the hands of those with dark intention. Hitler served humanity as a stereotype of the fallen angel … the Annunaki showcase. Given the way things play out in the polarity of Earth's reality, it is not that difficult to imagine why the secrets have been hidden right where you would least think to look — within your own walls. It is such an obvious place to bury a code: your DNA, the intelligent architect and container of the Knowledge which lies just as infinitely within you as you believe it beyond. Not even the words of the Illuminated Masters — the Buddha and the Christed One — were enough to point the way, for you could not imagine your own divinity. You were trained to look outward to the gods for your miracles — always reaching for the pot of gold. Did you realise that the myth places the 'gold' at the end of a rainbow? Consider the spectrum of your light, your chakric system, and you will have located another key to unlocking the treasure chest.

And what about the great chamber beneath the Sirian effigy, the Sphinx, guardian of Giza? There lies the vibrational trigger that is needed to retrieve the ten strands of DNA that have been stripped from you by the Annunaki, when they threw the grid around the planet. That trigger is soon to be fired, and once the secret is uncovered the alchemy will begin. But only when enough of you reach the level of awareness required to reintegrate the third strand of DNA will this key be turned. Once you understand how this works on holographic planes, your desire to physically penetrate the illusive chamber will disappear. Indeed, in your zealous search to solve the mysteries, beware of entering that vortex on any level, as only the Coded Master will be capable of releasing the keys to the archives and you have many obstacles to overcome before She can show you the passageway.

The enigmatic Sphinx figures also on Planet Mars in the Cydonia region of that planet and, as it symbolically mirrors the Earth sculpture, you are already exploring the link recognising the synchronicity of the Martian sculpture's appearance at this moment of your awakening. What you have yet to uncover is that there lies below the Martian Sphinx a multidimensional doorway that is a safeguard to the activation of the Giza chamber, and the One Coded Master will link up the third element of the triangulation with these two vortexes. She has already been given the codes of entry and is being prepared for the Grand Opening. She is preparing to help lead you back into the light and, guided by the light emissaries of the higher realms, has been actively preparing to serve that purpose for many thousands of Earth years. It is now, as your solar system enters into this dynamic phase of its transmutation, that she will turn the Sirian keys to universal ascension.

Please bear in mind the esoteric wisdom of the axiom 'As Above, So Below', as we draw your attention to a level of interpretation which we feel you must contemplate regarding the chambers and constructs lying beneath the Giza Plateau of Egypt and the Cydonia region of Mars.

As a result of your stellar origins and your subconscious longing to return, you give relatively little thought to what goes on below, be it within your own bodies or that of Gaia. You feel the earth beneath your feet as a physical certainty, a boundary, while tending to interpret the beyond as an outward and upward extension of yourselves, star gazers, ignoring that beneath and within you is every bit as endless and vital as the infinite vastness of the galaxy.

You pray to the four directions of North, West, South and East (the horizontal, lunar sense of place), often ignoring the vertical, solar plane representing the directions of above, below and there where the intersection or cross is made with the two-dimensional concept of centre — the direction of **within**, the absolution of balance in the radiance of the soul's light. You must adjust your altars now to honour and vibrate to the seven directions:

North
West
South
East
Above
Below
Within

Your government-controlled scientists have found a very convenient justification for denying life in the galaxy, by simply analysing atmospheric conditions of other planet bodies and applying Earth's biological formulas, concluding that no hospitable environments exist outside of Gaia. Considering that their explorative capacity is still limited to very few of the planets in your solar system, this is erroneous from the start, because it does not take into consideration multidimensional levels and precludes that life would have to develop above the body's surface. Below the surface of many celestial bodies throughout the universe exists an infinite number of civilisations with all their complexity and diversity of form.

Life below the surface of Gaia is abundant with colonies that have peopled many layers for millions of Earth years. The concept of life below the surface seems to boggle your minds and yet, you are well aware of the species of the animal kingdom, the reptilians and insects which penetrate and burrow into her caves and crevices. Do not forget that she is full of underground rivers, canals and wells — and have you not ascertained that the essential requirement for life is water? Most interterrestrial beings require almost no light to survive and, although sunless life is inconceivable to you as star children, it does exist. The capacity of life to adapt to environmental conditions and mutate into new forms is one of the most profound examples of your own immortality.

Neither should you overlook the fact that most of your more developed countries' governments have created elaborate underground tunnels, bases and military launching zones, many of which are already populated and have been manned successfully for many years. Others serve as future evacuation stations for the world leaders and military élite as part of the contingency plan should a third and final world war destroy conditions for life upon the surface.

Do you suppose they know something more than they are telling you?

You are remembering Atlantis at this time because you must now expand your vision to include possible realities that you have ignored or forgotten. The Lost Civilisation did indeed exist in three-dimensional reality, first upon Earth's surface and later below it, and many of the mutations created through their genetic experimentation still populate the below of your planet — in the same breath we remind you that your biological laboratories exist mostly underground. You are reliving the Atlantean scenario now, are you not? By drawing this parallel you will spark your ancestral memory, because it was from the Mars underground station that the invading Annunaki planned their invasion of the Atlantean civilisation and further, we declare to you now that below the Martian surface an entire civilisation exists … and the Secret Government is well aware of that as well.

The Mars structures have finally been identified and some of your most brilliant minds are charting the galactic maps. The Cydonia landscape is being paralleled to the triangulation of Stonehenge, Avebury and Glastonbury in England and this is, indeed, a great breakthrough in your cosmic vision. You have begun to penetrate the geometric patterns of intelligence sculpted into the landscape, and as Sirian sacred geometry reveals the multi-dimensional parallels, the secrets of Mars will soon be unveiled.

Referring again to surface consciousness and the seven sacred directions, we draw your attention to the Great Pyramid of Giza. Its four-sided pyramidal form is actually one half of an octahedron; it reflects the male vibration as it points facing the Sun. The other half of the octahedral form, the pyramidal female, extends downward, pointed at the Earth's core: the etheric mirror of the form above. Because your perception of the Pyramid has been largely limited to the study of only one half of its entire etheric body — i.e. the top half of the octahedron — you have never been able to truly decode it, nor imagine why or how the Egyptian elders went to such great lengths to create it. The superficial structure — the yang half of the whole — has held your fascination, while the mystery of Egypt's most impenetrable secrets lies in its unification with the yin reflection that lies below. This is the Wisdom, as it is shown to you again and again, manifest in your sacred symbols: the T'ai-chi T'u, the six-pointed star, the lingam-lomi, sun/moon, the tree of life.

If you will now visualise the structure's etheric reflection reaching into the earth and meditate upon the completed geometric shape of the octahedron, as well as the corresponding representations of the directions contained within it — you will facilitate your understanding of the true function of the Great Pyramid which is a free-energy prototype that was created to serve the conscious beings of Gaia throughout time immemorial. You, leaders of the Aquarian Age, are being gifted now with the keys of Sirian geometry, which will allow you to harness the energy of the accelerator at a time when you are releasing yourselves forever from the limitations of your three-dimensional cages.

It is extremely important for you to recognise the octahedron as the geometric representation of the seven directions. The seventh point, that epicentral intersection at the centre, the within, is the etheric heart and soul of the Great Octahedron. It is the quintessential Tibetan dorje: diamond par excellence, the inner geometric form of the interlocking star tetrahedron.

Perhaps you have never known to search for the heart of the Great Pyramid because you have been looking with physical eyes and listening to the wrong music.

We draw a correspondence between the position of your crown chakra and the location of the King's chamber, or the 'transporter room' as we shall refer to it, since activation of the Pharaoh's pineal gland was required before the activation of the Great Accelerator could be completed. Positioned in the vehicle of the granite 'sarcophagus', the Pharaoh would utilise the merkaba activation principle to set the etheric female pyramid (magnetic) below the Earth's surface spinning in a clockwise rotation. At the same time, the etheric body of the male (electric) material pyramidal structure above would be activated in the counter-clockwise spin. As the vibrational pitch reached the frequency resonant with the *wam* (the musical note) of the Pharaoh, it would draw the etheric magnetic pyramidal form upward intra-dimensionally into the electric male in counter-rotational movements, until the force of these two interfacing fields then sucked Gaia's kundalini fire spiralling up from her core, through the energy channels of the corridors — catapulting the Pharaoh through the dimensional barriers of your time-space continuum, much as your own bodies explode in ecstatic spirit fire when the flame races through the conductor networks, activating your chakras and then illuminating at the crown. That is the true function of the corridors; your understanding of these passageways as indicators of initiation levels is only partially accurate. The very name, 'pyramid,' (from

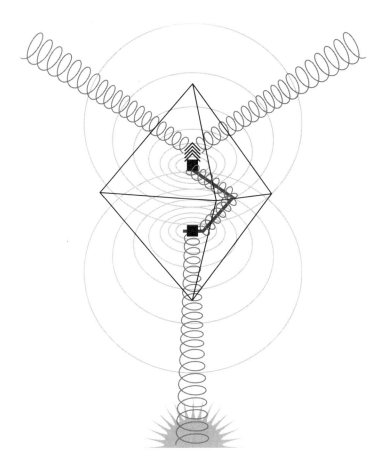

The Great Octahedron of Giza

the Greek: pyros=fire; mid=middle), describes that process, but without the completed picture of the Octahedron and a greater awareness of the etheric, you could not possibly make sense of your three-dimensional world's most impenetrable mystery.

The secret to the process of materialisation (descending back into body) then involved reversing the process, so that now the electric male spun out clockwise and the magnetic female form its reverse, into an counter-clockwise spin. It was the pull of the forms separating from each other which caused materialisation to occur, thus the Pharaoh returned from his stellar visitations back into his granite chariot.

Granite, incidentally, was utilised in the transformer for a very specific reason: it combines the elements of quartz and feldspar, both minerals known to you as conductors of intergalactic intelligence. The porous nature of this mineral conglomerate acted as a conduit which harnessed the rising energy of the fire, once the merging of the magnetic/electric halves of the Great Octahedron had reached its climax.

Sirian technology was carried to Earth by the Annunaki and the early Pharaohs, Keepers of the Records, all knew the secrets because it was their legacy. Let us suggest that the Pharaohs inherited the knowledge that allowed them to utilise the Great Pyramid in much the same way as you use your rockets. It is just that they transcended the physical limitations of space, while your astronauts are apparently bound in form, but this is only because your governments have still not pronounced themselves. As we mentioned, you are only spoon-fed what the Secret Government believes you are capable of absorbing, as it is convenient to their global strategies and private interests.

UFOs (as you currently understand them) utilise the merkaba principle: that of counter-revolving fields of energy merging into each other. Much will be revealed about spinning disks and rotating energy fields in the next few years. Know that of the actual sightings of craft now being seen in your skies, many are experiments of your own governments and are a result of their interaction and exchange with alien technicians. Others are holographic images created to bridge with your mental bodies, to prepare you for the merging of multidimensional realities as the entire solar system moves into position.

If you understand the free-energy model, you realise that there is no need for spaceships. The film maker, Gene Roddenberry, creator of the legendary Star Trek holographs, was a channel who showed you this and many other principles via the safety zone where you allow yourselves to play out probable realities as science fiction — but we assure you that there is nothing fictional and everything scientific about dematerialisation. This light bearer was serving your higher purpose on his mission for the time he spent in body on Earth, and his work accelerated your ability to perceive and accept extraterrestrial intelligence as a projection of yourselves, in what you currently understand as the future.

The Great Pyramid on Mars is a five-sided structure. It joins with its etheric underground complement of an additional fifteen triangular planes to form an icosahedron, the Platonic solid representative of the element of water. It, too, is a functioning energy transformer, but at this time you are still not evolved enough to comprehend its utilisation of reflecting ethers and light-bending through its sound reverberation chambers.

You must take one giant leap at a time.

Photographs taken from the highest government sources, your own spacecraft, also show sitting on the Martian terrain a number of four- and three-sided pyramidal shapes — yet these irrefutable proofs of intelligent life beyond your world have barely made the late night news. Much is being done to discredit the work of those who have risked personal loss and professional humiliation to bring truth to the public, and you are treated like gullible children if you dare to believe what your eyes perceive ... what your hearts know.

Projecting out from the landscape of Cydonia is a number of coded messages: 'There is life on this planet; there is water and we have the free-energy accelerators.' Once you have thoroughly investigated the superb work of correlations now being made, you will discover parallels to the Giza plateau structures as well as the megaliths and ley lines of Britain.

That intelligence must have at least temporarily inhabited Mars is boldly evidenced in the landscape of Cydonia, yet your space engineers refer to these stunning images as 'optical illusions'. They prefer to draw your attention to their spectacular discovery of bacterial fossil forms embedded in what they have named the 'Martian meteorite', alluding to the potential of some pre-existing condition for a most elemental form of life on Mars. Come now, Earth people. Doesn't this insult your intelligence?

We invite you to question why they deliberately distract you with such banalities, just as we encourage you to rebel against the disinformation which continues to hold you in isolation. Now is the time to reclaim your birthright as members of the Greater Family, your true ancestry ... a family far more advanced and alive than fossilised bacteria have ever dreamed possible!

While the majestic Sirian monuments and their sixth-dimensional portals gaze boldly out into space, you are being directed to focus upon a so-called 'Martian rock' — allowed to contemplate only remotely the possibility of bacterial life existing beyond your Earth. We will reiterate that there is indeed intelligent life below the surface of the red planet, as on Earth, and that your power élite have known that since mid-century, back when the scientists Tesla and Einstein were receiving open transmissions from alien intelligence on how to construct a free-energy accelerator. Their experiments are extensions of that knowledge, for since your second global war we have recognised the emergency on Planet Earth, and have been actively projecting to humankind the particular technological capabilities needed to help you ride out smoothly the rough edges of the next twenty Earth years.

Such knowledge has been yours since well beyond the walking of the Pharaohs, as far back as Atlantis, when mindlight generators illuminated the domed cities and pyramids of your ancestors and the Priesthood time-journeyed to other dimensions, other worlds.

We have come to help you remember.

Five

THE GEOMETRY OF
MANIFEST CONSCIOUSNESS

You are beginning to comprehend and experience that your being, as well as that of Gaia, is made up of many interpenetrating layers, and that your astral bodies can and do constantly separate and merge with other dimensions. Similarly, your solar system, indeed the entire material universe, is composed of various etheric layers and it, too, experiences out-of-body journeying. While your scientists struggle with the philosophical implications and scientific possibilities of parallel universes, they are far from understanding the concept of universal bodies and the etheric double of that physical universe which can move and interact freely with other dimensional realities and other universes, as does yours … more noticeably when you dream, meditate and project astrally.

We do understand that it is already a Herculean task to conceptualise the enormity of a three-dimensional, seemingly infinite material universe from your perspective. Therefore, we do recognise the difficulties you encounter when attempting to imagine it as the physical manifestation of a much greater, multidimensional living being, especially since your own multidimensionality eludes you. To further complicate matters, the term, 'layers', does not adequately describe the etheric substance of Universal Being, since the concept in itself implies a certain three-dimensional perspective of distinctly separate aspects. Yet, for our purpose it is necessary, as we are attempting to reduce into comprehensive language the workings of Universal Being's material, etheric and astral bodies.

Consider the sea of the material universe as a physical body, or rather, the manifestation of matter as constructed from the conscious will of Prime Creator. As quantum physicists have finally acknowledged, the source of matter is consciousness; that is, your scientists are now beginning to understand how matter forms when quantum waves are activated by consciousness. The prime mover, thought, defies the speed of light and it is only when it slows to that velocity that matter is potentiated. In a sense, then, we can tell you that matter is the result of thought slowing first to the speed of light and then light slowing further as it moves back and forth in interpenetrating patterns to finally crystallise as matter.

In essence, we are saying that Prime Creator first conceived of your third-dimensional galaxy as a receptive sea of consciousness manifesting itself through wave patterns which, activated, resonate in distinct geometric patterns. What appears to be random, or invisible, is actually an exquisite lattice of geometric form, proportion and vibration, laced throughout the material world. We can say that the architecture of matter then, is structured upon waves of consciously directed energy, forming in a fluid, constantly changing matrix of geometric proportions and harmonics.

It is the organisation of these patterns that realises matter in its endless dimensions and manifestations. If we are to accept that the entire three-dimensional universe exists as various densities of consciousness-matter, then by definition all that is contained within it shall be described as such. That which appears as a boundless sea of nothingness, a void, is actually a physical being which expresses itself in endlessly altering geometrically formed patterns of consciousness. Is it possible for you to visualise an infinitely connected universe of patterns and waves that are absolutely interdependent? We are telling you that your every thought affects the patterns of all reality.

What you first consider to be a void, upon deep reflection, is anything but that. For example, when you contemplate space you tend to imagine a dark silence, and yet you readily accept that within the void are celestial bodies, stars, space dust, asteroids, meteors, satellites, your space junk, astronauts, clouds, gases and other bits and pieces — including the mass of life and its manifestations on your very planet! Many of you have accepted the reality of spacecraft from other worlds, mother ships of enormous configuration and particles of other dimensions yet undefined. You may have heard mention of space bacteria, a rising concern in the scientific community. Let us not forget cosmic rays, gamma rays, and the sounds emanating from this space matter, and you will admit it is a very full void indeed.

The waves and particles of quantum physics are the elemental vehicles of consciousness, the stuff of which the substance of the universe is formed, much as amino acids are to protein. Nothing is independent. No matter how distant or separated things appear in three-dimensional viewing, all dimension, consciousness, dark and light are but polar aspects of the One. Therefore, when you are told that you can affect the outcome of all realities, be it an aspect of your individual world or that of the coming transformation due in the wake of Gaia's liberation, know that you possess the ability to alter any destiny. As co-creators, you continually focus consciousness to change frequencies and, in so doing, alter matter and affect time — or future time, as you still understand it.

If you drop a pebble into a pond it will cause a gentle ripple in the water's surface, while a boulder will send a wave crashing over the banks. We remind you that the universe is unfathomably immense and infinite, and so to effect massive change you must move past your sense of individuality and unite with others, consciously guiding the destiny of Gaia and sending those loving, directed vibrations on out into the vastness of Universal Being. Ripples of consciousness, however distant, are experienced in every dimension of Universal Being's soul bodies. This is why we are so involved in serving humankind at this critical stage of our mutual evolution. The waves pass through us and become our vibration, affecting our lives as they do yours, just at different frequencies of intensity.

And then there is the Gossamer Web, that brilliant unfolding of the golden light strings of Spirit, which, as the quilting of pioneer women of centuries old, is being interwoven from the outer reaches into the centre, and in joining, unites the Spirit Light of Love in all its dimensions and throughout consciousness. The triangulation of the light filaments, that most sacred of geometric forms in the Cosmos, embodies the creative explosion of the Trinity, and is the highway of the Family of Light ... the road home. At those junctions in the Web, whereupon the three rays meet, are radiated throughout the bodies of Universal Being the colourful spectral rays of your rainbow, and that is truly the bridge of mythic lore and indigenous peoples. We share in our mutual experience of spiritual awakening through the Web, scintillating with the music of the One Heart, the great *wam* vibration of Universal Being, and it is upon these strings that the Music of the Spheres is sung. The primordial orchestra is but the heart strumming the chords of consciousness.

Here lies the solution to the apocalypse scenario, which denies your godliness and negates your power to focus consciousness to the positive outcome — for your believing it creates it, as the waves of fear and impotence alter the very substance of the universe. We are calling you to unity, that you may raise the vibratory frequencies of your thoughts and reconstruct the universe to resonate with the hope and ecstatic vision of a brilliant, loving world, and those waves of love we will experience and reflect back to you across the Gossamer Web from our dimension of the soul body of Universal Being.

We have taken our instrument in etheric body out to the furthest reaches of your galaxy, simply by resonating to her *wam* and drawing her over the quantum waves to her stellar home, where she has received the vibrational attunement necessary to decode these transmissions. She has known the splendour of the journey through the vortex passageway into that etheric body of your galaxy, where she has connected with those of parallel universes at higher levels of consciousness. We are aware that it tests your credibility when we attempt to describe the enormity and complexity of simultaneous realities in simple, linear thought structures, yet believe that you, heart links of Alcyone, are prepared now to accept these truths as they are brought through to you via our instrument, Trydjya, one of the many messengers sent to assist in your retrieval of the keys of ascension.

To explain the multidimensional Universal Being, and how it folds and unfolds into its etheric bodies, we would create a metaphor of the volcano and its eruptive activity. As the molten, gaseous inner world below the surface reaches the explosive, yang phase of its vibrational body, it races through the volcanic vortexes, filling the space known as 'air' with particles of its form. Then, upon being pulled back down to the Earth by her yin magnetic force field, it runs back to the oceans and land formations to cool and crystallise, taking new form as the 'surface'. In essence, you witness an outpouring of matter through a vortex which, in a sense, then returns to itself in altered form. With time, as in the case of Atlantis, earthquakes, continental shifts and sinks cause these land masses to return to the below, and in so doing, complete a revolution on the wheel of the Earth's infinite cycles of transmutation of form and energy.

Your scientists are far from understanding the purpose, function and form of the black holes which permeate the Cosmos because, once again, they are working from within a three-dimensional framework. We, however, are not, so we are free to offer a quite different perspective than that which results from scientific hypothesis — one which you will need to contemplate and process through your intellectual and emotional bodies, to determine if it rings as truth within you.

The spirit of your expanding physical universe pushes through its vortexes, journeying along astral planes, to experience its higher dimensional selves, as well as the parallel universes which coexist as deity bodies of Prime Creator. Described to you as 'black holes', the vortexes through which the evolving soul consciousness of Universal Being passes are actually curvings of space, spiralling energy torus tubes which defy all laws of physics currently available to you. Your modern scientists want to define a black hole as some point of departure, where matter somehow leaves the material universe, without even venturing to explain where it then goes. Similarly, if science would wish to describe a white hole as a point of resurgence of matter, would it not have to define from whence it emanates, given the foregone contradiction that in leaving, it has gone 'nowhere'?

The white hole, then, is that vortex through which an aspect of the soul consciousness of Universal Being returns to its material body. In both cases we are basically describing the silver chord, that connection between the astral and the physical which you have either experienced personally in your out-of-body journeying or are now reading and hearing about from those who are having near-death experiences and astral visions.

It is in this cyclical rebirthing that your galaxy is continually being renewed, and we remind you that the birthing process is always a passing from one form into another, through the sacred darkness and the light and back again.

Think of the magnitude of what we are asking you to envisage: the evolving soul consciousness of Universal Being leaving its physical body through the tunnels of its astral chords to journey to other dimensions, other universes, other states of consciousness. Would this immense hypothesis not appear just as immeasurable and unimaginable to the consciousness of an atom of one of your cells, were we to describe to it your own astral voyages? And what is the purpose of it all? The answer is obvious: that just as you as a unit of consciousness seek spiritual enlightenment by overcoming matter and your limited physical perception, so does Universal Being, by ascending into its astral body, experience the apotheosis of its God-self, the renewal of *The All-That-Is, That-Has-Ever-Been and That-Always-Will-Be.*

The first Pharaohs, descendants (in every sense of the word) of the light-bodied ones of the Pleiades and Sirius star systems, enjoyed and relished in the pleasures of the sensate world and for this reason they developed with such intensity and focus their capabilities of preservation of the physical form, as manifest in their sophisticated methods of mummification of the body. Surely you must find this an interesting paragon. There you are, feeling 'stuck' in 3D, exercising your desire to move into your light bodies, while they pursued fervently the desire to retain the physical body in an immortal context.

Quite simply, observing your reality from our perspective is much less labyrinthine than your attempts to achieve the higher awareness and vision required to experience this dimension from within the density of 3D. Yet, you are developing these abilities and it will not be too far in linear time when you will know the merging of these multilayered realities. You are straining to imagine what lies ahead of you, and although you can not yet perceive it, you feel it drawing near. Things are moving faster now — moving much faster — whirling towards the great vortex.

You may now understand with greater precision the purpose of the Great Octahedron: the free-energy accelerator. The early Pharaohs, having achieved physical reality while retaining light body consciousness, wished to journey to the higher dimensions in body, just as they were intent upon retaining their form in death. Proud gods, they brought to the realms of the Pleiades and Sirius the experience of expression through dense matter, reflecting the higher frequencies of material existence back to the light ones of many dimensions.

Their intensified emotional bodies, polarised by Gaia's electromagnetic duality, sent waves of immense love, desire and pleasure to the Pleiades, the heart chakra of the universe; and to Sirian consciousness came a fertile field of new equations, challenge and probable realities to make crystalline and bring to form.

The seeding of Egypt was one of the great experiments of the higher dimensions, and all eyes were then focused upon Gaia, as once again, we have turned our attention to the great awakening of your world. Once again, do we feel and experience your love pouring out into the heavens and with the Pleiadian/Sirian alliance that has now taken wing, we wish to stimulate your stellar memory of the sacred geometry and form of sixth-dimensional awareness, united with the love of the Pleiadian vibration — that you may send the music of your souls across the waves of universal consciousness and know Prime Creator in every moment of your existence.

Orphans, you will feel no longer. Your galactic family longs for the moment when you shall be reunited at the celebration of Gaia's liberation and freed of your three-dimensional constraints. The grid that once held the Earth in the darkness of Annunaki control simply cannot withstand the frequencies that the Web is sending throughout Universal Being and besides, they are tired of their experiment. They have looked into their test tubes and found that the nature of hybrid human consciousness has altered the outcome. Finally do they recognise the no-win finality of trapping you in the extreme polarity of their intended controls. As Earth moves towards illumination the game is all but lost.

The descendants of the Annunaki, the power élite, feel the control slipping out of their hands, the grid disintegrating and the light winning and they are clutching the power for their very survival. An extensive strategy has been elaborated and put into place to prevent you from aborting their mission, and for this reason they have recreated a form of the Annunaki structural cage in the Internet, the techno-grid to which we have referred earlier.

Designed to appear as the ultimate communication network of humankind, the can't-do-without-it technology of the 1990s, is instead a quite dangerous control tool of the power structure. We know ... many of you love the Internet, as you are free to play and share your thoughts, knowledge and curiosity with brothers and sisters across the great expanse of your planet in instantaneous time — for you so long to be freed from your linear time constraints. You are promoting yourselves, establishing contacts and breaking down old systems with great zeal and delight, as you admire your advancements and celebrate the trends of high technology. So many of you are creating your pages for the Internet, joining with lightworkers from the world over in every moment of this most exciting of your times. You experience the infinite access and connection that it provides as a vital and positive step — a necessity — for your journey into the light. However, we ask that you consider carefully our vision of the techno-grid, for we believe that you need an objective picture of its far-reaching implications, and from the sixth dimension we perceive a quite different scenario than the one that is playing out in your minds.

Not so long ago, in your earlier technological phase of development appeared the radio, and life for you was never to be the same again. Gathering together around your new toy, you delighted with the voice of world news and entertainment, becoming receivers of consciously directed sound waves which you were free to perceive and interpret on many levels of understanding. You created visual images in your minds, experienced new emotions, and began to know what possibilities of global communication lay before the whole of humanity. A limited but effective tool, the radio altered your perceptions, manipulated to some degree your choices and affected your emotions — here was the first tangible form of mass mind control in your experience. Nonetheless, from the silence of your distant fields and still relatively remote populations, it was a welcome friend on those lonely nights of your isolation.

Television was the next great step to your gradual disempowerment. Now your imaging abilities and creative visualisation were stripped from you, supplanted by holographic images and sounds that reach out to you from your viewing screens. The Power now had an enormous advantage over you, for with this vehicle they could control you emotionally, market you, drug you and alter your lifestyles completely. Glued to your sets, stuck in your growing powerlessness, you have been exploited through television with quite disastrous results. Physically, they are making you fat and lethargic, while filling your auras with electromagnetic pollution, negative thought forms and addictive entrainment. You feel frustrated and bored, and, if 'nothing good is on TV', you become irritable and unresponsive.

And what about the children? They are losing their creative innocence, the delight of discovery in nature and simplicity, and are becoming anaesthetised to violence and despair. Haven't you noticed the dramatic increase of child suicide in your cultures, nor wondered why such growing numbers of youth are opting to leave by taking their own lives? Children are spending so many hours before the TV screens, left to wade through the inane imaging and violent disturbance portrayed there, that it is a wonder to us that they manage to move beyond it at all. Their small and precious bodies absorb such excessive amounts of radiation that you can be certain to see overwhelming numbers developing quite severe television and computer-related illnesses by their early twenties. This VDU syndrome is already appearing as chronic fatigue and manic depression in the first wave of television-raised addicted adults. Incidents of seizure have also been occurring more frequently in children after hours of computer elaboration, much to the perplexity of the doctors, who have no understanding or training in treating subtle energy manipulation, video syndrome and the effects of electromagnetic radiation. They have no idea how to treat the symptoms, much less the cause, for few want to believe in dangerous side effects from video entrainment. With alarming rapidity, the afflicted children will become more in number until you are shaken enough to rebel against your obsession and **unplug**.

Do not overlook the many billions of dollars spent in television advertising, where big business blasts product and interwoven subliminal mind control messages into your subconscious with such ferocious campaigning that you simply cannot resist on any level. They know a lot more about the impact of covert images, messages and sounds than you. Subliminals in the ads, such as print-overs, planted images and soundtracks laid under the overt message, attack your lower chakras — and soon, unbeknownst to you at a conscious level, you are buying product because your sexual, animal self has been stirred into action at the subconscious response level. This is fact. Although most advertising firms deny their use of subliminals, you can easily spot the material in many of your display ads in magazines, billboards and other fixed advertising.

Face it. The Corporate Earth Management Team sees you as mindless, controllable sheep who can be easily lulled into consuming, reacting and behaving as they wish. You are sold to believe you are not beautiful enough, thin enough, rich enough, smart enough or chic enough. Meanwhile, the products that purport to give you the beauty, body, wealth, intelligence and stature are constantly, unnervingly shoved into your awareness in every moment of your viewing. The ads are not only present in the official promotional text. They are interlaced in the perfect bodies of the starlets; a label caught in frame; the make of an automobile … it is all quite deliberate and well thought out. You have no idea of how much money and time is spent creating these image packages — for the agencies' work, their objective, is to guarantee increased sales to the client.

To that end, most corporate management will utilise any means available if they intend to remain in the highly competitive business of moving you into buying product. Advertising finances television, the vehicle that, until now, has most effectively moved masses of humanity to compulsive and irresponsible consumption. It renders you passive and receptive to political and socio-economic dogma, product and opinion. The more hours you watch, the more you subconsciously conform to the messages and, more importantly, the more you **consume**. They have the technology; you cannot escape it entirely, but you can greatly reduce the effect of subliminal manipulation by releasing yourselves from the instruments of mass persuasion and telecommunications.

The boom of the computer industry really spiced things up for the technology teams, for now you have must-have hardware and software which is immediately obsolete and they have a colossal, inert population positioned in front of a computer monitor or TV screen for the greater part of its waking hours. Considering computers in the work environment, home and schools now mirror the television addiction, that can easily mean that you are spending over twelve hours per day entrained by video imaging. Do you still believe that such technology is 'saving you time'? Be honest: if you have not yet unplugged, ask yourselves how much of your precious time you spend staring into screens? When did you last take the time to walk through a forest or a field of grass? Have you ever lain with your children in a bed of wild flowers in a meadow, or shown them the gentle breeze of the wind upon the waves? Most likely, your children are so entrapped by technology that they prefer a computer games room or sitting TV-glued to that kind of discovery, for it is too easy, and they, too, are becoming addicted to their inertia.

Used as an extension of your creative intelligence, computers do serve, and we do not wish to suggest that you return to some primitive state of existence, denied the benefits of technology. Rather, we would enlighten you to the dangers and misuse of that technology, whereby you become entrapped and disempowered by its existence. Herein lie our warnings about the Internet; we ask you simply to consider the negative impact along with the seemingly beneficial aspects of this grid, for that is exactly what it is. Now that fibre optics are being laid around the globe you can conceptualise the material reality of such a grid, but do you recognise the subtle implications that are held in its etheric formation?

You are beginning to believe that without this Net, you cannot be a functioning member of the Age of Technology. You believe that you are saving time, cutting through tedium with the arm of the Internet and are also convinced that if you do not become Net-efficient you will fall into some nebulous category of antiquated, ineffective mind where you will no longer be able to function in society. Many billions of dollars are spent to assure that you continue to believe in your dependency upon technology, and those same billions come right from your very own pockets. Ironically, it is you who are fuelling the mechanism in a self-perpetuating legacy that has you feeding the monster that keeps you in bondage.

If we may play out a sinister hypothesis for the sake of rousing you from your convictions, we suggest that signing onto the Net renders you interactive in many ways that are not in your best interest. The Power acquires the capacity to track your contacts, habits and buying capabilities. There is no end to the information you give away in your naïveté, for you believe in the Net and the techno-god, and indeed you have been programmed to do so.

Soon, all vehicles will be programmed through the Net. You will no longer need to study routing, read maps or rely on your natural sense of direction, for 'autonet' — disguised as a helpful location device — will actually be tracking exactly where you are when you are not online in your home or office. Satellite tracking devices for automobiles are already infiltrating your markets, being sold to the unsuspecting under the guise of 'theft protection' technology. Do you recognise the potential here? What would have occurred in the darkness of the McCarthy regime in US history (a brief fifty years ago) had the Internet already been operative? Do you actually believe that no one would be interested in accessing you for less than altruistic, constructive purposes? Given an elementary understanding of target marketing and statistical advertising, isn't it probable that some organisation is very interested in the kind of influential statistical data that will come from millions of Net users and their patterns, needs and buying preferences? Certainly, there lie a number of interesting possibilities for at least commercial exploitation, given the built-in mailing lists and user profiles. Do you recognise just how vulnerable you are rendering yourselves and those with whom you are electronically interfacing when you are exposed in your entirety through the wires?

One step further now, let us suppose that dark forces would wish to once again suppress and persecute lightworkers, spirit leaders, holistic healers and any free-thinking, creative individuals whose work or interests could be considered threats to the system. Do you think about this, or have you forgotten the days of the Holocaust, McCarthyism and the Crusades? Your memories are short. What could be more penetrating and targeted than calling up the great data banks of the Internet, and simply searching the pages of organisations and those individuals who, as lightworkers, offer services and alternatives to that which the corporate control team mass markets out to humanity? No longer underground, those of the light are dangerously exposing themselves in the Net, intricately caught up in that mechanism like flies in the spider's web. Yes, Internet appears quite a remarkable invention, and most of you will defend it vehemently, arguing that it saves time and the high cost of conventional communication technology, opens new horizons and reaches the unreachable.

We are asking you to exercise caution and objectivity regarding your need for the Net; above all, recognise that your obsession with time has, in the end, bound you for long hours to the computer screen. We question whether or not you are being freed as you think, or are simply redirected to another illusion of the meaning of time — the fourth-dimensional element that eludes your comprehension.

Coded into the grid of Internet technology are subliminals more powerful and manipulative than those of the television and advertising networks. There is a powerful pull coming from your monitors that is created by highly sophisticated methods hooking you into the system, which utilise buried and coded messages perceived only at the subconscious level of your minds. There is also activation of sound frequencies imperceptible at the conscious level, which creates an energy entrainment from which it is extremely difficult to release. Unfortunately, your understanding of the human mind is still limited to the function of a very small part of the so-named 'grey matter' that composes the material brain. It is still relatively unknown to you how the subconscious can perceive information and experience stimuli while the conscious mind cannot. This is a great danger to you.

If we appear to be overly emphatic that you understand the mind control methodology of the power structure, it is because they have initiated a ferocious, all-out campaign to exploit you from now until the great shift that will be experienced on Earth and out through your entire solar system. We wish to serve you by stimulating your awareness, so that you will be able to resist being embroiled in their nets. Our instrument, Trydjya, has been tuned to pick up the emanations from the mere reading of a printed Internet document, and she is able to recognise that the etheric essence released from reading such material already has the magnetic pulling force within it. Gazing into the screen is far more hypnotic, far more damaging and this is one explanation why so many people now admit to being actually addicted to the Net.

There are inaudible sound subliminals emanating from the grid, far beyond your conscious range of perception and these are actually filtering through the fibre optic underground cables and into your units. These cables are being laid through your city streets and connect directly into your homes, schools and offices, and their purpose is to grid you once again in control netting through sound technology and other advanced mechanics to which we have alluded here. If you are sceptical about manipulation through sound frequencies, we call your attention to a recent event in political sabotage when the American Embassy experienced mind-controlling sound frequencies and electromagnetic emanations being beamed into its Moscow offices. It made news, but you know too little about this type of energy manipulation to respond and react to its implications, and it was presented in such a way that you believe it belongs to the world of James Bond and cannot touch you personally — so you tune it out.

We are concerned that you understand how and why these methods are used, and later learn to perceive these frequencies at the conscious level, for once you have brought the information up into consciousness, you can no longer be manipulated by it. Aware, you can learn to deflect the waves back to the emitter, clear your energy bodies from their effects and release yourselves from control mechanics.

In no way are we suggesting that you fear your technology, for we do not encourage fear within you, but rather ask you to awaken to the possibility of mind-control technology within this framework and, therefore, we suggest that if you must utilise the Net, then do so discriminately. Prepare yourselves by first encircling your being in a force field of golden white light, which you will then visualise surrounding your computer, penetrating into the circuitry and the fibre optics of the system and finally out and into the receiving computer of your target contact. You must intend that your instrument be capable of scrambling the high frequency sound waves coming through the equipment, and that you be shielded from any subliminal information being beamed through the screen. This is an absolutely necessary preparation before you work at the Net. In so doing, you will not only be partially shielding yourselves, but will also be releasing on some levels the mechanisms of control programmed through the system, contributing to its disarmament. Nothing, however, will be as effective as simply not becoming a user and remaining 'offline', if we may quote your hi-tech jargon.

We will warn you now, however, that autonet is the missing link in the ball and chain that you will place around your freedom. Given our elaboration regarding controls and electromagnetic emissions, we are suggesting that you not allow yourselves to be stroked into believing that you will only be able to find your way when guided through the Internet mobile circuit. That would truly be a statement of total resignation and brainwashing, and we already know how they will manipulate you into believing that you are 'nowhere' without it.

Wouldn't you say it is about time you built up some sort of alarm system against techno-exploitation? As members of the dawning, you must be clear regarding this issue. Yesterday's technology marketing objective was the mass introduction of Internet at the personal and business computer terminals; now begins intense commercialisation of interactive Internet/television hookup. Autonet has begun to appear in a more harmless version of computer-assisted mapping for your convenience while driving, and is already being proposed as an option on the latest model luxury cars. There are laboratories quite ready to insert computer chips into the neural networks of your bodies, rendering you mentally robotised and physically 'track-able'. They would have you implanting biosoftware directly into your brains — biological computer chips covering any of a number of subjects — and education as you currently know it would disappear, as would natural intelligence. Do not fool yourselves into believing that this is some ranting fantasy, for cyberbionics technology is the right now of the industry, and don't think you aren't being slowly prepared to accept it, too, as 'progress'.

Certainly, you are alert to the implementation of artificial organs, for many advances have been made in that field, and some are very positive. We are more concerned with organ and gene transplants, precursors to biocomputer technology. Many of your governments are enforcing legislature which allows the state free access to your body once you leave it, to be utilised in the profitable medical application of organ transplant surgery. Rest assured that each cell of the body is a fully conscious reflection of your soul vibration, and by imposing your etheric blueprint and physical tissue into another body they are absolutely violating the laws of divine creation, interfering with your mutual karma and denying your soul its unencumbered journey back to the light. A fragment of your being remains inexorably attached to another, and the soul destinies of both are permanently altered.

Much of this type of interventionism occurred in Atlantis, and we have already alluded to the monstrous mutations created by gene transferring and other unnatural biological experiments, including organ transplanting. These processes do not serve the highest purpose, and are another example of how seemingly humane technology is actually operating contrary to the higher order.

Some of you have developed your awareness and sensitivity to recognise the music of your soul — the *wam* vibration. At some level, you feel and experience every cell, indeed every subatomic particle, as you play the vibration of your soul essence through the waves of your being and out into the sea of existence. Transplantation of donor organs cannot but create atonal discord within the body of the receiver, for in the subtlety of vibrational frequencies which remain beyond your physical three-dimensional realm, the whole has been interrupted … the music disrupted. The donor, whose *wam* is retained as a remote vibration in the body of the other, remains trapped in the hinterland of the grey zone between Spirit and matter, light and dark.

The human body, house of the soul, follows a predetermined, unique pattern of soul expression created to fulfil certain karmic requirements which you set before entering. DNA, the intelligent architect, establishes the geometry of the physical body (as determined by species, race and genetic memory), and so the bones, tissues, fluids and organs carry the soul through the physical incarnation — subject to your free will intentions — from inception to the passing. That period of time where the body still vibrates energetically, although declared 'clinically dead' (a questionable status determined by forces outside of the free will individual), does indeed still carry the song of the soul and, therefore, the body must be left in sweet silence as the transmutation reaches finalisation. By the time the music has ceased in the tissues and fluids of the body, it is no longer feasible to perform organ transplant surgery — this is the danger zone. In essence, if the organ holds enough life force to be transplanted, it still carries the soul frequency and must not be disturbed.

Your spirit-manifesting body never intended to be artificially attached and superimposed into the vibrational blueprint of another being, whose desire (imposed or otherwise) to cling to the physical life denies the soul process originally set forth before incarnating. Indeed, it most surely didn't anticipate a government simply mandating free access to your soul and denying all free will in the matter. This is absolutely contrary to the laws of karma, and does not serve your higher purpose. It is also highly indicative of your present misconception and fear of the death process, which is still largely viewed in your modern world as the **End in Finis**. The transformation of matter is the beginning of new form and the natural process is that the entire being, a conscious, physical expression of life, experiences in its entirety the dissolution of the physical as a normal process of its own evolution.

Death, then, is to be perceived as passage … a continuation of existence and the evolutionary experience rather than the end of life. From seed to tree and then to seed returning.

Six

SACRED TEMPLES

We have alluded to the importance of healing the physical body and the clearing of toxicity and blocked thought forms that you have held within you. Know that your quickening to the higher frequencies will be greatly determined by your ability to release the excess energy trapped within the body, which you experience as disease, un-wellness, emotional upsets and quite specifically, eruptions in the stomach, breathing apparatus and skin.

The closing of the Piscean Age has brought a greater understanding of the true meanings of well-ness and dis-ease, as many of you are now turning to more holistic methods in your approach to healing the physical. We note that more and more of you have grasped the basics of creating the state of right mind and emotional balance, so that disease and disharmony do not have an arena in which to form on any level. As you are learning to recognise the physical form as a product of the etheric body, so are you developing the •knowledge needed to work with the mental and emotional bodies to prevent discord from materialising as illness, and are once again (as in Atlantis, Tibet and Egypt) utilising the vibratory waves of light and sound to equalise the electromagnetic body. Once you fully accept that all creation is the materialisation of conscious thought, you will move to a higher level still where the healing process you are rediscovering today will no longer be necessary — where harnessing the mind power of the individual for personal and planetary harmony will be as simple as the striking of a tuning fork is to creating sound.

This, as Gaia prepares for full planetary ascension, is paramount if you wish to remain in body, since energy blocks held within any layer of the being will prevent you from riding it through. Put simply, those with malfunctioning bioelectrical meridians and energy shut down will not be able to withstand the enormous energy shifts and the intensification of photonic light now coming into play as Gaia moves to centre stage in the galaxy.

The year 1994 was a pivotal time-frame for your solar system. It marked the acceleration of Earth's transformation and the awakening of the other celestial beings of your sphere. Jupiter was galvanised by means of manifest bombardment from deep space, which stimulated that body at a rudimentary level of physical life and then reverberated on out into other realms, unrecognisable in biological terminology. However, the thought forms of beings connecting with the Jupiterian vibration have been reactivated, as all prepare for the shift. Those of you who experienced Jupiter's shock treatment in your emotional bodies are particularly tuned into those multidimensional beings, for you resonate to that expansive, liberating archetypal energy. Therefore, you are well aware, if even at subconscious levels, of the shake-up that is coming to the three-dimensional realm of planetary reality throughout your entire solar system. If you can imagine kundalini fire running from your Sun through every planet body of your Solar Deity's being, then you may be capable of intellectualising and anticipating the awesome light waves that will course through the galaxy and ripple out to the farthest reaches of the universe in what we can best describe to you as a galactic orgasm.

So now it is essential that you rapidly heal those blocks that prevent the harmonious flow of energy through your electromagnetic bodies, for you cannot even begin to imagine how these electrifying photonic waves will race through your chakras: something like shooting 50,000 watts through an electric toothbrush! As with Jupiter, the entire solar system is currently experiencing a cosmic tune-up, and at this moment we are observing the explosive opening of impressive numbers of human beings. Bear in mind that each unit will be responsible for its own evolution, for that is the free-will choice of every individual. Many will choose to leave, unwilling to let go of the addictions of the sensate realm, and that must be, for it is part of the natural process. Those of you who do wish to ride out the great waves of change must at this time consciously undertake the alchemical task of metamorphosis, known to many as the Great Work, or the awakening of the light body.

We have alluded briefly to your food, but wish now to elaborate on a specific approach to changing your eating to facilitate the transmutation or alchemical reaction within your physical bodies. Clearly, if it is light that you wish to create within your form, what better source than plants? These are the lungs of Gaia, and as a food source provide not only oxygen to the system, but draw light into the cells. Know that every cell of your body is activated by light; like a miniature battery, with north and south poles; each cell holds within it the full rainbow spectrum, just as you have come to know the colour spectrum of your primary chakras. This is an important clue to understanding the importance of the axiom 'you are what you eat' as a commitment to the soul on its journey upward.

Here is the alchemical magic that has eluded all but the greatest adepts throughout Earth time: we bring to light now the primary formula for the awakening of the light body, although the information has always been there for you, right under your collective noses. Plants, you understand, capture light in their leaves in their photosynthetic process; the ingestion of raw fruits and vegetables draws the light through the digestive system and most significantly, through the darkness of the intestinal tract — reacting within your cellular make-up as light bearers replenishing the *Ka*, or life force, within you. Your more industrially advanced cultures have greatly misunderstood the spiritual significance of food, which is widely used for aesthetics, pleasure, emotional gratification and habit. The key here lies in understanding that food must also be taken to replenish the light frequencies needed by the cellular units of your body.

Your life source, your energy, is light, which enters the body through the skin, the eyes and, most importantly, your food source. As you have become more removed from the earth by your technology and commercialisation, you have abandoned and forgotten the true meaning of nourishment from the food supply, which must feed not only the physical but also the spiritual self.

Regarding your approach and understanding of food, we note with concern the tendency of many to cook or process the life (the vital light) out of fruits and vegetables. We are telling you that the essential chemicals needed not only for the perfect function- ing of the body but also the opening of the pineal gland are found primarily in raw fruits and vegetables, grains, nuts and seeds. Raw and unprocessed, these are perfect light-bearing foods from the very bottom of the food chain, just as nature intended when you were so close to the soil of Gaia that you understood. Here are the simple principles you will need to adopt with some urgency into your food awareness in preparation for the acceleration:

- eliminate dead animal flesh from your diets.
- eliminate artificial colouring, flavouring, synthetic foodstuffs and synthetic vitamins.
- select wholesome, unprocessed, natural foods from the bottom of the food chain such as grains, seeds, fruits, vegetables.
- radically change your methods of preparing food to include from 60–70 per cent uncooked vegetables and fruits ideally straight from the tree or plant source.
- eliminate microwaves in every aspect of your food consump- tion.
- seek biologically grown produce or better yet, grow your own. Plants respond to the heart with even more light; all living beings flourish with love.
- incorporate seeds, beans and fibre into the diet.
- bless the foods you do ingest and encircle them with light.
- silicon dioxide can neutralise some of the contaminants found in your drinking water: place a quartz point in a glass bottle and store filtered water overnight before drinking.

Will you consider the eating of raw, green large-leafed organically grown vegetables as the drawing of light and life into the body instantaneously? Seeds, particularly those of the sunflower, are among the most beneficial food sources; for in their concentration they contain very high frequencies of light and provide substantial nutrients and biochemicals to the body. Consider nuts, seeds, and beans as the least processed or chemically altered of the foods available to you. They carry light into the bloodstream and through the black tube of the intestine, strengthening the *Ka*. Learn to enjoy seeds and nuts in their natural form rather than toasted, salted and processed in chemically altered oils and seasonings which destroy their pure nature. Food that is flavour-enhanced is almost always chemically processed, and that destroys the light.

Organic gardens will become essential to your process in this next decade, for the pesticides used in the mass production of fruits and vegetables create toxicity in the body, and in a sense negate any benefit gained from their ingestion. Bear in mind that if the food is appealing to an insect it is most likely healthy for you, so do not be concerned if a few creatures are found sharing a lettuce leaf or tomato. Their presence is a sign that the food is clear of toxic pesticide and waste, and you would be wise to accept them as *messengers*. Much can be accomplished in your organic gardens to distance the insect community by way of select plantation. The planting of garlic sprouts around the perimeters creates an olfactory boundary which many insects find offensive and refuse to cross; you have also seen the consumption of raw garlic as an effective protection against mosquito attack. Garlic, the miracle food, serves as one of the most potent natural disinfectants for your systems, and it performs a number of functions in maintaining balance and good health.

Meat, we wish to reiterate, is devastating to the body, mind and spirit. Consider that you are taking violent death into your being every time you cut into a piece of meat, and remember that it is old, dead flesh that you are feeding a body you wish to enlighten. Do you see the irony of this contradiction? You are bombarding your bodies with the adrenaline overload of the terrified dying animal — hormones, toxic chemicals and genetic tampering utilised to artificially stimulate growth for the obvious reason of increasing the yield. We won't frighten you with details of bacteria and other living organisms feeding off the dead carcass, but you may want to consider that as well. Moreover, you are sending darkness and density into the system: lead ... not gold.

The eating of cloned animal meat, only just around the corner, will introduce complicated genetic mutations into your bodies, and you can be certain that it will glue you further down in density. We are suggesting that dead meat, the darkest foodstuff, is most clearly going to plug up your digestive systems, so why not eliminate it? Once you recognise its density as an obstacle to your work on the light body, you will hopefully discover that your desire for meat has simply disappeared. Many of you have already noticed a developing lack of interest in meat; what you may not have yet identified is that this is a stage of your species' evolution.

And what of the use of sound and light in the healing spheres? Throughout your history — and with that we intend that which is recorded and well beyond, from a time when the continents were one land mass — sound has been utilised as a great catalyst by the beings who seeded Gaia and their descendants. It is appropriate to this time of your awakening that you understand the power of sound in opening portals, releasing energy, altering matter and clearing the way to ascension. In the ancient civilisation of Atlantis, before the Nebiruan vibration had disturbed the harmony there, the beings were highly receptive to sound, and they experienced the music of Gaia coursing up through the soles of their feet as the 'bass chord' of their identity. Every planet, indeed every dimensional layer, vibrates to its seed sound, and so the beings of Atlantis, descendants of other worlds, brought to the Earth realm their cultural identity in the form of sound ... for you must know that Atlantis was a multi-ethnic culture of many civilisations that had come to pioneer the New World. It was a time not unlike the seeding of the Americas, just that the immigrants were beings from many dimensional levels and star systems beyond the terrestrial plane.

Each soul held its own musical frequency, and its infusion with the music of Gaia created a sort of individual soundprint throughout every cell of the body, which we have referred to as the *wam*, or the soul's music. Harmony among the beings of Atlantis went well beyond emotional interplay, for at that time in that civilisation one could hear the soul music of the other; and as all music in some form or another flows into itself, there was no discord. As such, that prototype Earth culture was deemed one of the greatest successes in the galaxy, a place where multidimensional beings attuned to the Gaian vibration in peaceful coexistence, and greatness was achieved on many levels.

As time passed, the three-dimensional vibration of sensate reality and the gravitational pull of Gaia began to interfere with the individual *wam*, knocking it out of tune, and healing would become necessary. This was accomplished in the crystalline caves of Atlantean shores, where the healing priestesses would attune the *wam* simply by striking the appropriate crystal matrix and creating a resonant tone that would bring the individual back into harmony. You are remembering the use of crystals in healing now, but still have much to learn about the use of the musical keys of crystals, for it is ever-so subtle and most of humanity, bound to the third dimension, no longer hears the music of the other.

Intervention from the Annunaki in later generations threw off not only the subtle individual vibration, but so powerful was their aggression that the sound frequency (the *wam* of Gaia) was thrown into violent discord, much as it is today. With the force of the omnipotent warrior, they harnessed the Priesthood's knowledge of sound and crystals at such a devastating frequency that they could detonate sound like your current bomb warfare, and we remind you that sound warfare (Annunaki methodology) is still being utilised to control and dominate. What you have yet to learn about the destruction of that continent and the ensuing inundation is that the disturbance of the sound frequencies of Gaia is what upset the balance on the planet, and here we are offering you **yet another key** to the understanding of what holds your world together — and what will once again shift the sands.

Three of the High Priesthood of Atlantis escaped the final devastation of that continent to reach the shores of the now Himalayan mountains, where they established the knowledge of sound and sacred geometrical form. At the flourishing of the Atlantean civilisation, the beings who populated that immense island were operating in multidimensional consciousness, and that is why there is some confusion regarding the material reality of that land. Atlantis in its many generations did indeed exist in 3D, and if its significance is now surfacing in your memory it is simply because, since your procession into the Aquarian Age, you have begun to rediscover the secrets of your antecedents at the same time that the so-called junk DNA is being retrieved … bringing you to full consciousness as galactic beings inhabiting the blue-green planet. The Akashic memory, your personal journeys and an overview of the projected future become One in the awakening, accessible to you now that the veil of darkness is slipping away.

The Three of the Himalayas agreed to preserving for future generations of Gaia the knowledge of the music of the soul, but it had to be camouflaged from those who, as in Atlantis, would abuse the energy to control and distort the frequency — much as had occurred with the synthetic crystalline forms of Atlantean advanced vibrational technology. Their legacy to that slowly evolving culture was first the implanting of sound portals, which could be opened only when the soul had reached resonance, and then the use of Sirian geometric forms as sacred gateways to the higher realms. These symbols are interwoven within the architecture of many structures of Tibetan mysticism, appearing throughout the art of the temples in the form of mandala and geometric sculpture. They hold the frequency of a time when the musical vibration joined with sacred form to open the portals of time and dimension in that culture. Unfortunately, the knowledge has all but disappeared from that powerful vortex with the Chinese invasion of this most sacred of your twentieth-century cultures. The Lamas have fled from the snow-covered mountains of Tibet, escaping the tyranny of the dictator, and most of the knowledge and the sacred tools have been removed from this holy land. Few remain who truly understand the power of sound upon sacred symbols, left in effigy of a time when humankind held many of the keys.

The first Tibetan masters, descended from the Atlanteans, developed a way to reproduce and preserve the *wam* externally by creating certain sacred tools, which include the dorje, the bell and the Tibetan singing bowl, a most sacred object which carries within its overtones the *wam* of the master for whom it was created. These symbolic tools were, at that time, carved from minerals extracted from that rich earth, a carry-over from Atlantean crystal wisdom. Later they utilised the seven and nine precious metals which correspond to the chakras — the musical keyboard of the *wam*. For many generations, the more highly developed spirit leaders of this civilisation had such mastery of frequency that, much like the Pharaohs, they were able to journey in body to parallel universes and were frequent visitors to other dimensions. By activating the frequencies embedded in the bowls, they could also experience simultaneous lifetimes as soul consciousness throughout the experience of their Earth lives and others. The music of the soul remained alive in the mystical bowl, a form of Bodhisattva available to assist whosoever had developed the ability to retrieve that inaudible frequency from its physical manifestation released in the playing of the instrument. Many of you who have come into contact with the singing bowls of the Tibetans, although enchanted by their mystical beauty, are unaware that you actually hold access to the soul music of the Tibetan masters which resonates out to you on many harmonic layers and waves. A very special few have the memory, and can activate the bowls at the *wam* level, and these are the gifted channels amongst you who are preparing now and will soon be called upon to join those indigenous peoples (localised in strategic geographic centres around the globe) in holding the *wam* of Gaia as she moves into her higher octave.

Mastery of sound has been exalted in many civilisations of your rich history, and the knowledge is still with you, governed by those light ones of certain native beings such as the Maya, the

Indians of the Americas, the Dogon, the Lamas and the Dolphin Beings. These are united in holding the Gaian vibration and unfortunately, it is also held by the power élite, who would once again abuse the knowledge to hold you in their controls. Like the Dark Priesthood of Atlantis, the Power has the ability to detonate the vibration. Their warriors have neither love of Gaia, nor respect for life and humanity, and they are still intent upon trapping you in the darkness of your ignorance — where they have attempted to hold you throughout the Earth time following their intervention in Atlantis. As we have intimated, sound manipulation is an essential part of their technology. While lightworkers are uniting to reverberate with the music of existential Earth fields, the power is running the new grid of control frequencies right below your feet, further anaesthetising you from your primordial ability to hear through those chakras — raping Gaia's rich soil and mineral beds with the chords of their insipid devices. Once again, knowledge of sound and its awesome power is teetering between the poles of light and dark, as are you, in the pre-dawn of your transformation.

What do we intend when we speak of harnessing sound to alter matter? You need only to gaze at the Great Octahedron of Giza or the ancient walls of Machu Picchu to recognise that your bewilderment over the movement and positioning of such gargantuan monoliths is justified. Standard archaeology dismally fails to explain how mortals of those 'primitive' societies could possibly have transported, pulleyed and raised such colossal structures. In the case of the Great Octahedron, the perfect masonry — monumental granite and limestone blocks often seamed at less than one millimetre — denies establishment tales of Nubian slaves driving through the relentless sun of the Sahara on sheer muscle power and the whip of the master. To relegate such behaviour to the evolved civilisation of Egypt is to diminish the legacy of one of the most significant cultures of human history, and certainly denies the overwhelming evidence of support from galactic beings, present at that time in Gaia's evolution. Minimal sensitivity to the energies of Giza can only affirm that a great spirit, mysticism and humanity lie in the higher consciousness embedded as thought forms and energy fields in the subtle crevices between the blocks of the Great Pyramid. Nowhere will you find buried in the mortar the rage of toiling man — the supposed slaves of Egypt.

We confirm the hypotheses of some of your new thinkers. Indeed, the work of these structures was a simple and effortless joining of mind, whereby the powers of the Priesthood were called upon to set the sound frequency that would be required to elevate the blocks. They held the Atlantean knowledge of the power of sound, as did the Maya in their similar works ... and the Tibetans, who utilised their understanding of sound and the human voice for the higher purpose of holding Gaia's soul vibration, which has indeed held the planet together for many, many millennia.

The Dolphin Beings are highly evolved entities whose material-isation on Earth was realised as a part of the soul incarnation of Gaia. Their light mission in the evolutionary theatre has been to monitor the frequency of the oceans. There too, sound holds it all together, and we assure you that the recent decrease in their popu-lation has everything to do with the exacerbation of the raging waters of *El Niño*. Your study of ecosystems has yet to elaborate the significance of sound upon balance, yet the Secret Government knows. Have you heard about the strange mutilations in the bodies of the Dolphins, whose recently washed-up corpses disclosed gaping holes drilled up under the throat, into the voice mechanism? Like a science fiction drama, the power élite are attempting to har-ness Dolphin sound patterning. They have been performing experi-ments upon the Beings' sound devices in an attempt to acquire and utilise the knowledge, but their bungling of that exercise is upsetting the dynamic tension of the oceans — which will cause the departure of the Dolphin clan, who are beginning to suicide. Highly evolved Light Beings, they cannot be manipulated to serve the Power, so unless you move to stop the dark work of their exploitation you will soon witness massive death in your seas.

Be warned. The loss of the Dolphin Beings and the great

whales, who have already been slaughtered to near extinction, will mean the end of the balance and the final destruction of the ecosystem.

Seven

CLONING AND THE GENETICS NIGHTMARE

———————

You must also confront, at this time, the ethics of biogenetics, an issue that first stirred you to question the sociological implications of your future technologies with the arrival of Dolly, the man-made lamb. Soon after the Dolly debate, news broadcasters presented you with triplet cloned cows, and already your indignation had waned, tempered with the promise of new proteins and medical miracles to be created from genetically tampered milk. Sooner than you think you will be ingesting gene clones in your Rice Krispies, for this is somehow, at some level, received in your consciousness as an acceptable application of the technology.

We encourage you to recognise that hormones, chemicals and genetically restructured proteins from your meat supply and milk are not health inducing in the human body. At the risk of being monotonous, we urge you to wean yourselves off them now, before this practice has become standard in animal food products, rendering them far worse for you than they already are.

More ominous than the cloning of animals is the eventuality of cloned human beings, which you are being prepared to accept as well. Consider that only a short time ago the world gasped in indignation at Dolly; however, once the mass mind was adequately drugged into acceptance and resignation over her existence, the mad scientist, Richard Seed, appeared out of nowhere announcing his intention to pioneer cloning of the human being. It is our observation that you are slowly letting this, too, seep into your group consciousness — while accepting it on a subconscious level despite your resistance, which becomes weakened as that reality settles deeper and deeper into the waters of your subconscious and sets anchor within your minds.

What possible benefit could be derived from cloning your-selves? Is your fear of death and your attachment to the physical, sensate reality so all-encompassing that you would want to fix your own immortality in some artificially reproduced, generational rebirth of your seed? The contemporary suggestion that additional body parts could be grown in a clone to provide available tissue in the event of a needed transplant is grotesque by any standard, and yet this is one of the more widely proposed applications of the cloning process.

Do you understand what is involved in cloning? In simplistic terms, the nucleus of a cell of the original body (container of the DNA) is isolated, removed, and then transplanted into the stripped embryonic egg of a mother carrier. There, it gestates and hypo-thetically grows into an exact replica of the original blueprint — the artificially created being.

Scientists suggest that one of the significant medical appli-cations of cloning is to be able to grow yourself a failing organ, tissue, or other biological material in the event that you find you require spare parts. You are being sold that this is a potential application of cloning, along with other promises of genetic break-throughs, miracle proteins and cures of the formerly incurable. As to the idea of physical immortality and cloned organs, we do invite you to follow the absurdity of such thoughts out a bit further. Are you going to allow yourselves to be convinced that cloning back-up bodies of living beings (however artificially induced) would somehow be ethical if it were to mean extending your own physical lifetimes? A cloned race of beings, then, to be eventually violated and dissected as biological warehouses for some future need that your true Spirit bodies — those godly soul creations — could one day require to artificially prolong the lifetime?

Suppose you could grow another and yet another still … would you then simply continue to add decades to your lifetimes, so that you are projecting your physical realities for generations, while postponing indefinitely your return to the light? Choosing to remain in physical reality, we assure you, is true condemnation for the soul, which longs to return to Spirit. And yet, the scientific proponents of cloning have mounted just such a campaign and you are slowly seeding (Richard Seed-ing) the idea in your group mind.

As you are being lulled into acceptance, they are already well underway in the manufacturing of cloned beings, and we wonder when you will play out that improbable future in terms of just what that would mean to the overpopulation crisis, Gaia's primary disease. Can you imagine, at a time when your world has exploded in uncontrollable overpopulation and is witnessing its catastrophic effects, a second layer of beings? Are you prepared to meet the needs of a futuristic clone generation: living, breathing soul-less beings requiring every bit as much space, food and primary needs as the to-the-limit existing population? Before even delving into the complex sociological implications of the clono-genetic nightmare, we return to our previous question of what purpose cloned life forms serve in your cluttered Earth reality.

Cloned babies? Your obsession with child bearing at a time when, globally, male sperm counts are dropping is understandable, and yet, as we have already explained, this is nature's way of correcting the imbalance. Can you envisage the psychological implications of raising cloned reproductions of yourselves? Try to imagine the insanity that would result from experiencing a carbon copy going through the process of your growing up all over again. Aren't you already psychologically traumatised enough in your parent/child dramas without confronting yourselves in **both** roles: mother and child?

Know that, if you are being told about the potential of a given technology, it already exists. You can be quite certain that human cloning was tested and proven technically 'successful' in laboratories well before it was presented as a futuristic possibility to measure public opinion. Just as the adept Einstein's vision mutated into a means of destruction, so will most humanitarian ideals of the potential of genetics be reduced to the lowest vibrations of human consciousness, once the ethics barriers have been stampeded upon and the scientists left free to play God with human life.

Those Atlanteans amongst you surely recognise this information, as a dissonant thought form wells up in your memory,
and you may experience fear but not surprise that it is happening
again. The later generations of that civilisation experienced these
mutations just before the sinking of the continent, and it is no
accident that Supreme Being brought the Atlantis project to rest,
deep in the healing waters of what has been appropriately named
the Atlantic Ocean.

You have yet to experience the horrors of genetic experimentation as was developed then, but unless your collective consciousness alters that projected reality within the next ten years, you will
know aberrations never imagined within the closing of the Mayan
time construct of 2012. The modern day alchemists (the new engineers of the DNA material) are intent upon creating the monstrous
perfect man, the ultimate ambition of your evil archetype, Adolf
Hitler. They are burning with the fire of the all-powerful knowledge of their discovery, feeling like gods, lords of the biological
realm. It is the Annunaki rape, once again, only this time the mass
mind is consciously aware that it is taking place and **consenting**.

You have already forcefully united sperm and egg within the
test tube, and do also possess the capacity to specify genetic codes
and make-up so, effectively, Hitler's dream is already well within
the reach of anyone with a substantial knowledge of biogenetics
and a relatively sophisticated laboratory. We observe your inability
as a whole to integrate racially and can only imagine what would
develop once a cloned race of predesigned, genetically 'superior'
beings began to take seed in your current states of separation and
your still unresolved male/female polarities.

The experiment will fail again, however, for man cannot override the Divine Plan, and his artificially created life forms will not
supplant the perfection of life as soul manifestation. Quite simply,
no enhanced intelligence or genetically manipulated biology will
ever improve upon that which is life consciousness in its natural
karmic cycle … life that lives out the incarnation as intended and
dies, or transmutes, just as the soul that sparks that life planned
before manifesting. Your modern alchemists are too young at the

game to know the distortions and freak creations that will evolve from their invasion of the natural process, for they are drunk with the illusion of mastering the secrets of creation. However, they cannot artificially reproduce the soul, and as such their microscopic bits of the puzzle may eventually piece together a basic physical form, but without soul consciousness there is no meaning to that life — no purpose. We are therefore talking about biological atrocities and soul-less shells who would further populate a suffocating, dying planet.

True spirituality builds upon a basic understanding and acceptance of the death process. It is the surrendering — the dissolution of matter as it transmutes into light — that is the key to the meaning of life on all dimensional levels. Many of your more spiritually advanced cultures, such as those of the Tibetan Priesthood, the Maya and the Native Americans, prepared for the death process from the first moments of their 'I Am' awareness. Rather than fearing death, they explored it, trained for it, so that the passing would be familiar when time called them back through the tunnel, the metaphysical reflection of the tunnel of life known to you as the birth canal.

It is the mirror, the identical process, except that the returning to the light is much less traumatic than the coming into matter. The death canal. One doorway leads in, and another leads out, only the 'in' door moves from light into the density of the physical passageway of the vaginal tunnel. The 'out' door, the portal of the liberated soul (as we mean 'freed from the limitations of the physical existence'), exists only as a multidimensional doorway from which the soul expands from the dense material back to light, releasing from the crown chakra.

Rather than desperately seeking to prolong life and resolve illness by means of artificial intervention, you are ready now as spiritually evolving beings, to learn non-attachment to the physical reality and the illusions of the sensate world. This will be accomplished when you recognise that your soul is eternal; it yearns to return to the light just as it seeks a return to form in the infinite cycle of karma and evolution.

Eight

TIME AND ETERNITY

Time as you experience it from within the confines of three-dimensional reality is a totally artificial framework. That is, your perception of time is based on a linear construct of some ambiguous past, an illusive, indefinable present and a future of projected outcomes that often cause you to be anxious and uncertain about your lives. In truth, most of your difficulties stem from your misconceptions about time, particularly now, at the turning of the millennium. You are beginning to attempt conscious awareness of the 'now' moment, of living it, but most of you are far from grasping that there exists nothing else. This is understandable, for the experience of no-time is of a higher realm beyond your present capabilities, although you do touch upon it in your dream states and out-of-body journeys — there wherever you escape the sensate world. For this reason is it so essential to your spiritual unfolding that you explore your dream material, meditate, and develop your abilities to project yourselves out onto the astral. There lie the greatest opportunities to release from your limitations and drift in the sweet liberty of timeless awareness and body-less motion.

From the higher octaves, what you perceive as past, present and future is viewed as coexistential and simultaneous. This is absolutely incomprehensible from the three-dimensional viewpoint, for your history — your very race consciousness — has evolved around a model of linear time. Yet, if you can recognise the no-time of multidimensional reality (if even only intellectually) you can be freed from past nightmares or memories of better times, as well as futuristic inventions such as the impending apocalypse of doom.

In rediscovering your light selves, you begin to integrate the concept of soul consciousness creating and recreating itself in body, which you are currently moving through past and future hypotheses you perceive as real; fearful and fantastic happenings that you believe caused your life to be as it is; or 'some day' events to be lived in nebulous time, which lies always just outside of your reach. Paradoxically, the past-present-future illusion is so credible, so seemingly tangible, that it is unfathomable how time can exist in any other context. As your lives are organised on that plane, you have needed the pseudo-structure of time-in-a-line — for it has pointed you, as a race, in the direction of the winds of change, both forward and back in your projection of the past and memory of your future. And no one is going to convince you that a tomorrow of sunrise, a first cup of coffee, the office and the myriad activities of daily routine are mere figments of your imagination … yet we dare to emphasise that it is so. There is nothing else but the moment. That is the reality, the experience. Moments within moments, forever imprinting upon the matrix of Eternal Mind.

Let us take as an example Benjamin Franklin, who appeared in Earth's linear time construct in the early 1700s, embodying what you hold in pride as the rich fibre of American history. Delegated to the past, his accomplishments are noted with reverence, for his knowledge and vision changed the very fabric of human experience.

From our perspective, the Master Benjamin is every bit as vibrant and alive in this moment, indeed much more so, as he was in that finite Earth time reference. His dedication and daring, curious intellect brought to humanity the elemental knowledge needed to comprehend the harnessing of the electrical frequencies of Gaia's electromagnetic body — driving civilisation into the Industrial Age. An ancient soul, he has brought the Wisdom to countless beings in many dimensions, and his teachings have indeed altered infinite realities. He currently resides here with us in the sixth dimension, a Speaker from this Council's scientific committee.

Are we asking you to accept Benjamin Franklin, great icon of American history, as an 'extraterrestrial'? Yes … in identifying him we are challenging you to reach past scepticism, recognising the infinity that lies just outside your perception; where a universe teeming with life holds the soul patterns of every conscious being that has ever existed, and where Earth is but a blue-green speck on the colourful canvas of the Cosmos. She is just one of thousands of planet bodies which compose the material universe, and on etheric planes there is simply no counting — so infinite is the experience of All-That-Is. We ask you to accept that not only are we to be defined 'extraterrestrial'. We are extradimensional, projections of your own consciousness in another phase of its multilevelled existence. We are telling you that the mind of Benjamin Franklin, the conscious focus of that manifested being's entity, contributes to these transmissions, and that that is no more surrealistic than the idea of our instrument picking up, decoding and recording sixth-dimensional frequencies to begin with.

In another aspect of your being you exist on these waves, and you, too, may send the currents of light to a receptive channel, at a level of your existence which you would currently identify as a future lifetime, but which we rather define as a higher stage of your evolution. Most likely, having been drawn to these teachings you are already, to some degree, serving that function both in three-dimensional and in different realms, to which you may or may not yet be consciously attuned.

We are telling you that what changes is the form of your existence rather than the time. Past lives, which for you are easier to conceptualise than future lives, are still perceived in linear terminology — while we wish to impress upon you that these extensions of your dynamic energy all occur simultaneously, racing across the cosmic seas as waves upon the great oceans.

Constant (however changing in form), the oceans of Gaia are infinite. Each wave, a reflection of the greater body, has its moment as one spectacular essence breaking upon the shore — then returning unto the ocean deep, it changes form. Yet, it still exists there. So do you, manifesting body in some constructed Earth time-frame, return to the cosmic sea, existing as soul vibration while donning myriad other aspects in simultaneous lifetimes which you create in the karmic unfolding of your journey.

In reference to the Master Benjamin, note that every time you read his verse or make reference to him on any level, a wave of light permeates his conscious field of experience, for that is how resonance functions. Consider that every time an electric switch is turned on, a cosmic light ascends the spiral and illuminates his aura — the gift of having served others. We assure you that no greater reward exists than receiving the light of love, for the purpose of all missions on our way back to Prime Creator is that of illuminating consciousness. The Master Benjamin is known as the Manifest Lightworker of Earth reality, and enjoys much notoriety on higher planes for that particular contribution to your development.

From a point of reference beyond your current possibilities, time is not a factor; that is, we experience your entirety as thought made manifest in matter, and every unit of consciousness contributing to the whole of your material existence. We access the Akashic record to bear witness to the uniting of that material egg (the sea of existential matter) with the sperm (the activated will of Prime Creator), and from that union comes the birth of the material universe. From our dimension, we see the complete lifespan — the birth and death of the material — as it then moves up the cosmic spiral into its next manifestation. We cannot foresee or understand our own higher dimensional realities, for that is the nature of the journey; but we do experience your world and physical existence as a Being, a wholeness, whose individual units of consciousness (like the cells of your bodies) live as matter for a particular time span and dying, eventually transmute into higher, less dense levels of awareness.

When you gaze into the mirror, you cannot discern the millions of cells that are dying and being born every day that your body lives. You see the entirety — the whole; it is only when the self begins the decline of the life cycle or threat of death that you contemplate your own mortality. In opening to Spirit, you are reminded of the purpose of that death, which is to return to the light and ascend the evolutionary spiral. So it is with the material universe, and the many bodies of its soul.

From the fourth dimension out you are into the higher realms, where all things and beings are consciously aware that they occupy the same space in infinity as energy exchanges that are constantly mutating and changing form, as is appropriate to soul purpose. We experience form as vibration, and as we have described quantum waves and particles, all is in a constant state of movement and variation. Therefore, the interconnectedness of all conscious beings in the material and non-material universe creates continuously every form and outcome, and time as you think you know it is not at all a fixed measure.

Here we need to include the aspect of etheric imprinting on the sea of matter in all its forms of density. We are telling you that at the etheric level everything that has experienced· existence, which we will define as 'thought', remains. Therefore, Supreme Being, so absolute in its aspect that we cannot perceive of its magnitude, is aptly defined: *The All-That-Is, That-Has-Ever-Been and That-Always-Will-Be*, and that is one and the same as the 'one moment' — everything exists right now, always has and always will.

One of the greatest keys of knowledge that serves you now, as you prepare for the shift, is the understanding of timelessness, which you experience when you leave your bodies. You are given glimpses in the dream state, and in profound meditation; we note that those of you experienced in astral journeying have a more profound awareness of the higher realms. Consider that your existence as human beings confines you by the very nature of your bodies, which move around in density in a very linear way. You go to school, to work; you get up and lie down, and so on; what you consider conscious activity is, in many ways, quite mechanical. From the unconscious perspective, the body performs hundreds of thousands of intricate functions instantaneously, yet you are obviously unaware of what enormous energy is required of your beings just to pump the blood, cool a fever or fight infection. Your healthy hearts, timeless motors, race through the entire lifetime never failing, never faltering ... that alone is one of the most miraculous aspects of your being housed in the physical body.

Similarly, you are quite unaware of your emanations, as they permeate the immediate space around you and further out, riding the waves of the sea of consciousness — formed of the thought of all creation. In keeping with the theme of time, we ask again that you recognise how every thought and emanation you send out into the sea is at once eternal and profound, resonating through the Cosmos forever ... for if there is only the now, then there is always forever. Somewhere at levels you have yet to understand, the group voice of your planet journeys to untold civilisations and permeates many layers of existence. This moment in Earth's reality — its convulsive revolution and the imminent ascension — is being broadcast through the waves, for Gaia is the communication centre of your Solar Deity's chakric network, and all who can hear are listening.

We shall call the metamorphosis that your planet is undergoing an aspect of the dimensional shift which will be felt throughout the universe, an immense moment in all-time for humanity as well as other conscious beings in the Cosmos. This is why so many from countless dimensions have opened direct contact, for we understand that you are making the leap in awareness which will enable you to bring in and process the information, as you must now prepare as a civilisation for the shift into the fourth dimension — a world beyond time, beyond illusion.

Long have we peered into the darkness of your density as you strove through the struggle to rediscover the light, and now is the time. We celebrate your awakening, just as we strive for our own illumination, for the journey never ends. Each unit of consciousness moves up the spiral as in some superbly orchestrated symphony, where every instrument — the lute and the drum — is vital to the playing out of the song.

We will focus now on zero time, that coming of the Christ for many, for others the birth of the Illuminated One — two points in the history of humankind that stopped the clocks. Of such monumental impact were these two events that time was to become point specific to their occurrence, so that the Asian calendar delineates time as pre- and post-Buddha, while the Christian calendar reflects the birth of Jesus the Christ in the same manner. That is, time stood still and then came to zero … a pause in the linear timeframe, where humanity knew in its totality the meaning of the 'now moment'. So great was the light of these Ascended Masters, so vast and profound, that much of humanity momentarily escaped the time barrier and experienced fourth-dimensional consciousness during the time they walked the Earth.

The Maya have provided the next zero-time reference point, for their galactic calendar places the end of time at 21 December 2012. As physical beings in linear time, you fear this ominous reference, for to many of you the 'end of time' is synonymous with the end of life, and we sense the fear swelling in your bellies as the clock ticks the countdown. Your understanding of this next key will serve to release you from the fear and move you forward in the light of your ascension:

The closing of the calendar
The end of time
will be a coming again to zero point…
your evolution out of the constraints
of third-dimensional reality.

Surely, you sense with bewilderment that something spectacular is about to occur, but your fears and Gaia's upheaval bring you to the doom. And so we draw now the parallel of other moments in your history when zero time heralded the shining of the light upon your planet, and we invite you to raise a glass to the birthing of the new dawn. Contrary to your feelings of dread and anxiety, you are not only ready for it, you need it … you have created it, for the pendulum has swung all the way out to the extremes of the poles and Gaia returns full centre in 2012, which is as much the past and the future as it is the right now of your existence.

There has been such speculation and theory regarding the fated date that we feel it of the utmost significance, indeed a primary purpose of these transmissions, to attempt to clarify just what is happening in the galactic picture in that point of time, so that for once and forever you may let go of your fear and experience your evolutionary processes with due awe and wonder. Conceptually, that which we wish to share with you will no doubt test your credulity, yet we ask that you push yourselves to the absolute limit, break the dam of conventional thought and set the flood waters of your imagination free to flow as possible realities upon the cosmic sea.

The Aztec Sunstone
Copyright: John Major Jenkins – Bear & Co. - Publishers

Returning to our earlier discussion of black holes, we do wish to validate portions of current scientific theory that describe (from the material perspective) how these vortexes result when a star evolves to a point where it simply collapses, pulling into itself as the force of gravity draws its particles to the centre. Remember, now, that in the vastness of Universal Being, a star is as infinitesimal as a cell is to your body, so you must operate from that sense of relative proportion to perceive of the death of a star as it is experienced by Universal Being, versus its impact upon all living things within its solar system. A collapsing star becomes more dense as it contracts, and all that surrounds it is pulled into its gravitational vortex, unable to escape the force of that gravity as it is sucked into the consolidating stellar body. Matter (as we intend it to mean manifest consciousness), time and space surrounding the star become altered, creating what the quantum physicists refer to as a 'curve in the time-space continuum'. As the collapse gains momentum, its gravitational force increases until it is so powerful that not even light can escape the pull. In such a vortex, light moves faster than the speed of light, and as such the entire tunnel appears as the blackest of all voids, if you are observing it from a remote point of reference, while the passing through as an active part of the experience is of a velocity so beyond your comprehension that there is no 'time' to experience that darkness. The astrophysicists who adhere to the general precepts of Einstein's relativity theory generally agree that the surrounding space begins to curve or warp as the star collapses, distorting time — and when the process reaches the phase of total collapse, time stops altogether. We suggest that where linear time ends multidimensionality begins, for you know that all deaths are but passages into other states of being, and all endings are new beginnings.

In our metaphysical approach to the phenomenon of black holes in space, which we have described to you as 'the soul consciousness of Universal Being ascending through its astral chords,' we have touched upon the same experience from the perspective of multidimensional awareness and the immensity of Universal

Being. That which your scientists postulate as a random event in the Cosmos we perceive as Soul reaching higher, which is the absolute principle of all existence: Soul at every level of co-creation reaching higher as it ascends the spiral. There are no coincidences at any level of existence, for all is in the state of perpetual becoming, and so it is with every soul body of every living being throughout the Cosmos.

This transformation of the evolved star, then, is just as integral an aspect of your ascension as is your personal evolution as consciousness units of the Earth realm. As a Solar Deity, it experiences illumination in the transformational process of condensing, collapsing and rebirthing itself into its higher dimension. From the macrocosmic perspective, the collapsing star is but an aspect of the material self which experiences transmutation, while providing a pathway for Universal Being to expand and experience its higher astral bodies. We realise how immense this appears to you, how far out of conventional thought you must reach to grasp its enormity, yet as you recall in the key — the macrocosm is a reflection of the microcosm. As was written upon the temple walls of the Eleusian Mystery Schools in Ancient Greece: *Man, Know Thyself.*

Where are we headed here? That is, how does it all link together? If you have been following some of the more significant events in your solar system, you are aware that your Solar Deity has been erupting with flares and violent explosions the likes of which have never before occurred in recorded Earth history, creating further instability on your planet. You may look forward to more extremes in weather, violent seas and powerful electrical storms. Many of you experience solar flares in your etheric bodies regardless of your conscious awareness, but now it will be important to pay more attention to solar activity, for the information we are giving you here is manifesting now as the preliminary stages of the Sun's transformation.

The collapse of your star, your Solar Deity, has begun and the process of moving through the astral chords of the black tunnel and into the light is about to take place. This is the galactic scenario of 2012: all celestial bodies, space and time surrounding your Solar Deity move out of the physical and into a higher dimension, experiencing as an entire solar system the death of third-dimensional constraint and birth into multidimensional consciousness. Indeed, you are already cognisant of the warping of time, as the pull of gravity drags you into the vortex, where you will race through the tunnel faster than the speed of light and emerge in the fourth dimension.

From a distant vantage point, as your astrophysicists observe stellar collapse of stars millions of light years from Earth, this appears quite a cataclysmic event. But from the eye of the storm, the transition is absolutely natural and will be quite exhilarating for all but those who are still clinging to the materiality of sensate existence. That is why so much information is being beamed to Earth now: methodology for the healing of the body and the release of miasma, thought forms and energy masses which prevent the flow of light through you, for you must be prepared to receive intensified radiation of photonic light in the process of approaching and emerging from the hole. What you now experience as sunlight is but the physical manifestation of pure cosmic light, which will course through your bodies with unimaginable brilliance and illuminate your souls in the ecstatic unfolding of this — your Solar Deity's transmutation. For it is not Gaia alone that transforms, and if we have primarily addressed only Earth's ascension until now it is because that is the celestial being with which you are the most familiar, even if of earthly things you, the human race, still know so very little.

Nine

ATTUNEMENT

Working in unison with our instrument's spirit guides, we have created the necessary openings for her to journey to key sacred sites on the planet; to attune her, to implant the codex, to stimulate further her memory and connection to those civilisations in other realms of her experience which we will refer to as other 'lifetimes'. An ancient soul, Trydjya has wandered the Earth for millennia, seeded in the star system of Sirius at a time when the lands of Gaia were one continent, known throughout the legends of your native elders as 'Turtle Island'. Her experience of Atlantis spanned many generations. In the first incarnation, Trydjya served as a healing priestess of the amethyst cave — a Keeper of the Crystals. She was assigned the safeguarding of one of the thirteen crystal skulls that have appeared and disappeared at various stages of your evolution, for they were bequeathed to humanity to be utilised at pivotal junctions of the advancement of your race. The second was a traumatic lifetime, when she was cast underground as overseer of the spheres … this, too, involved working with crystal frequencies. Her final experience in the Atlantean Priesthood came at the end of time for that culture, when the seas of Gaia washed over the island and brought it to rest in the deep abyss of the ocean, for the soul-less technological advancements of that time (which, we remind you, find direct parallel in this moment of your technological development upon Planet Earth) had humanity playing God with life.

Atlantis was truly the crystal hour of humankind's greatest potential and flourished for many generations … until the uncontrolled build-up of energy, the abuse of power wielded by the technology of the later days upset the balance, and all was lost.

Few survived the great cataclysm of Gaia's revulsion, so intense was the rage: so immediate and unrelenting. Those souls of Atlán, the survivors as well as the perished, have resurfaced at this time, to assure that the human race, seed of their seed, does not repeat the Error.

You, who have come to our message, have begun to remember.

Trydjya has walked through innumerable Earth lifetimes, serving and assisting in Lemuria, Egypt, Galilee, Tibet, Sumeria, the lands of the Maya and Mesopotamia — and has held vibration on many levels of dimensions still beyond her conscious awareness and comprehension. Her knowledge and memory of these and other lifetimes, like yours, lie within her DNA and are now being retrieved, and so is it for you ... for as you are being recoded to assimilate the third strand, you are reliving as memory the past-life scenarios of your many incarnations in the Earth realm. This is occurring now to facilitate your pulling up from the subconscious all the layers of your being that, as evolutionary triggers, have brought you to this moment. All of your experience is relevant, contributing to your understanding of what you feel you need to complete at this time in your process, and what you have come to learn in the university of your earthly education.

Here we are faced with a dilemma, for whilst we have asked you to accept that there is no time but the present, we are attempting discussion of the memory of past lives. How can we but not create within you a strong sense of contradiction? And what of future lives? If we were to tell you that we are the voice of your projected group consciousness travelling the waves of the cosmic sea, could you conceive of it: a future which is manifesting simultaneously in another dimension; your evolved soul-mind, whose voice is brought back to you through an instrument who is your contemporary — a physical being who currently resides alongside you in the third dimension? We realise we are pushing you, stretching you beyond your safety zones, and yet, that is the purpose of this book and these teachings. You must understand the fundamental workings of the universe (from the furthest reachings of the macrocosm to the infinitesimal subatomic particles of your bodies, the microcosmic blueprint) at this cardinal point of your evolution. You will be called upon, you the awakening, for soon you will be needed to teach the Wisdom to others. Those of you who now are drawn to the writings of our instrument and others like her will in turn become messengers of acquired truths, and others still will follow, for knowledge is the light of the Web. In the prophecies of your indigenous peoples, the caretakers of Gaia, time accelerates before coming to an end, and so do the individuals who have attuned to the Mother. Trust that you are where you should be, as you intended, in the now moment of the great evolution of your Solar Deity: in the all-time, the no-time … moving towards the end of time and beyond it, once and for ever.

While it is our intention to open you to the exhaustive possibilities of the 'no-time' framework, we realise our limitations and find we simply cannot override linear time. Our words reach you at the intellectual level, where you can allow the concept of 'no-time' as a possible reality; but there is no point of reference from which to experience it, considering you are trapped within linear time. Unless you dedicate yourselves to the discipline of meditation, with which you release yourselves from the sensate world and practice coming to *samadhi* (the state of timeless bliss), the illusions of your past-present-future simply frustrate your intellectual cap-acities to perceive the all-time. As you are trapped, so are we, in a sense, for in all learning there is a place of reciprocal knowledge and experience, and your being confined to the third-dimension limits our avenues of expression — our ability to establish that meeting point. We ask you to bear this in mind as we attempt to provide you with the keys to the time enigma.

When we speak of 'past lives' or 'ancient' civilisations we are, from our perspective, actually describing an entire panorama of simultaneous experience. It is no different when we speak of the future — the future of your Solar Deity, of Gaia and every being that comprises those entities — for (and we reiterate) what you perceive as a string of chronological lifetimes and fixed events, we recognise as consciousness simply manifesting at different co-ordinates in the time-space continuum.

Let us examine, in simplistic mathematical terms, your own scientific data regarding the illusions of time in relationship to light velocity. Consider that at the speed with which light travels (186,000 miles per second), light from your Sun requires approximately eight minutes to reach the Earth. We doubt that any credible astrophysicist would disagree with this elementary calculation, for it belongs to that world of information that your scientific community labels 'fact'. Where you may encounter resistance from some of the more conventional scientists, however, is in the disputed theory which derives from that information: that, given the eight-minute travel time required for that light to reach the Earth, you are essentially always witnessing the Sun as it was in the past — a Sun as it existed approximately eight minutes prior to your actual viewing of it (eight minutes later).

It will be strange to you. You have surely never given any thought to the idea of your Sun manifesting light on the Earth in delayed time, for it pours down upon you in the right now of your day. One might say you just take for granted the certainty of the Sun's presence, for it seems to be such a constant in your lives, and light is all around you for so many of your waking hours. You see the Sun rise as you rise and then set in the evening, in the twilight hours of your days, and this all appears to be occurring in real time — the illusive, misunderstood term which describes, in the end, simultaneous time. But the light which illuminates Gaia reaches you eight minutes from the moment it emanates from the Sun's surface. Can you imagine the possibilities of an eight-minute time gap from the time the Sun's light radiates from its mass to the time it reaches your planet? That means that, in the event of an explosion of devastating magnitude on the Sun's surface, the people of Earth wouldn't even know about it until after eight minutes had transpired.

The Maya were aware of the eight minute delay in the Sun's light journey to Gaia, for theirs was a highly intelligent civilisation which enjoyed direct interaction with multidimensional beings who brought them the knowledge of cosmic workings of the universe — which we have briefly described in terms of quantum physics. They understood the illusions of linear time, the process of death and rebirth and the existence of parallel universes.

Crystal skulls were utilised throughout that civilisation, placed in their astronomical observatories, pyramids and other strategic locations. The great Mayan seers, Keepers of the Crystals, were psychically attuned to the skulls, and as such were able to read the condition of the Sun and all other celestial bodies in **real time** — for thought, on the other hand, travels instantaneously. In essence, the skulls not only provided access to the galaxy as it was unfolding at every moment but also released the viewer from linear time — so that these very seers could look into the future and the past of all experience on Earth and across the heavens.

The purpose of crystal in ancient civilisations and specifically the mysterious workings of the crystal skulls has long eluded your scientists and archaeologists, whose encounters with these magical artifacts have been most unproductive and always will be, for we are talking about some of the most sacred objects in existence. Only the delegated Keepers can fully access them, although on rare occasions, gifted psychics have been able to unlock some of the entry codes and tap in. More is being discovered now as the native peoples come out of hibernation: they have waited for this time to come forward. Council of the Keepers of Gaia has already united, moving into leadership roles for the children of the Earth, and they will reunite the thirteen skulls in the secondary phase of the time warp. This too, was foreseen in the teachings of the elders and carried down through the oral tradition, psychic sight and intuition, as well as direct contact with star beings at various moments of our appearance upon your Earth.

Returning now to linear time-frames and our study of the speed of light; it should be obvious, given the simple calculation of light's velocity, that the further away the physical distance of a celestial body the greater will be the amount of time required for its light to reach you. Astrophysicists teach you that the brightest stars in your night skies are so many millions of miles from Earth that it takes years for their light to reach you. Think about that

simple statement for a moment; digest it and bring this key now
into full consciousness.

> **The brightest stars in your night skies**
> **are so many millions of miles from Earth**
> **that it takes years for their light to reach you...**

Doesn't that boggle your minds? Surely, when you peer out
into the starry canopy of your night skies, you do not consider the
possibility that you are actually observing stars and planet bodies
as they existed many years ago. So then, on the basis of that
hypothesis, it stands to reason that as you look upon the heavens
you are gazing at many stars, millions of miles from Earth, that
may actually no longer exist. In the process of their evolution they
may have already burned out, exploded, or passed through their
own astral chords in the death-rebirth passage. We are suggesting
that when you gaze into the heavens it is as if you are looking
through a time machine. What you see shining into your eyes and
the astronomers' sophisticated telescopes is the light of stars,
remote galaxies and the reflection of heavenly bodies as they
existed tens, hundreds ... thousands of years ago.

Just as you are staring off into the past every time your eyes
meet the light of a celestial body in space, so are other star gazers
who happen to live hundreds of light years from Earth — and
there are many, many populations of beings throughout the material universe who are doing the same. From their perspective then,
wouldn't they be viewing your present reality in delayed time of
hundreds of years from now? Let us invent a remote planet, which
we shall call 'Zargon', positioned so far from your solar system
that its inhabitants are actually viewing Earth as it was two thou-
sand years ago, around the time the Christed One entered centre
stage in your evolutionary theatre. Yet, in your reality, there you
are racing through the Technological Age, about to move the
entire planet out of the third dimension altogether. Or we can shift
our focus, projecting into the future where the Zargonians are
observing contemporary Earth at 1999; meanwhile, your entire

solar system has already moved up into its higher dimension and Gaia no longer even exists in the material reality.

Now, returning to our first example, imagine it all from our perspective as multidimensional beings who can observe the Zargonians viewing Earth at zero time of the birthing of The Christ, while at the same time witnessing the Earth of the impending twenty-first century and you will hopefully have an even clearer idea of what we mean when we refer to 'simultaneous time'. We are attempting to show you how time distorts in the material universe and, moreover, how time is not independent of space. Only when you move beyond the third-dimensional point of reference does it become clear to you and that, dear ones, is where you are headed when we speak of your passage through the black hole, through the astral chords of the universe and on to the next level of consciousness as an entire body of planets, stars and celestial beings moves upward in consciousness.

This is the glorious unfolding of *The All-That-Is, That-Has-Ever-Been and That-Always-Will-Be*, of which all life is a reflection — an aspect. From a simple stone along the river's edge to the most complex mental construct ... to the great celestial beings of your universe and beyond, we are but conscious units of the One, pulsating our vibrations through the sea of consciousness while receiving those that pass through us, breathing in life and letting out love — in a timeless continuum like waves upon the oceans.

This is the wonder of existence. It is the **Reason**.

Like Trydjya, many of you are being called to pilgrimage, for the process of your preparation (the awakening of your light bodies) requires that you integrate Gaia — the living Being — for she will provide safe passage to those of you who have accelerated. At her chakric centres, you have begun to gather to assimilate the energies and be activated and healed. Beware of the myriad 'openers of the star gates', those self-declared spirit warriors who are infiltrating your light centres and your communications networks, claiming to have come into the body on assignment: the single-handed activation of the sites. Be not misled; no one individual currently residing in the third dimension has the capabilities to single-handedly activate a sacred site. It is your group consciousness that, by concentrating light in those locations, revitalises the energies there.

Keepers of the Energy, those who can best direct your energies and facilitate your alignment through ceremony, meditation and prayer, are to be found in the indigenous spirit leaders who have had the knowledge of those sites handed down to them in secrecy, generation after generation, from the Wise Ones. Only now, as the time of awakening has finally arrived, have they begun to welcome you for they are no longer veiled in silence. They, the voice of Gaia, are emerging now — a voice that is reaching across the oceans and desert plains — and they are your direction. And so it is that now you are journeying to the far corners of the Earth seeking out the Keepers. You are coming into resonance with the power zones of Gaia, receiving her, and in the inviolable act of magnetic embrace are you finally coming to know the Goddess in her entirety.

In the energy exchange all is moving up ... all is intensifying. We speak of an ongoing, experiential process, which some of you are being led to by your own spirit guides. Also, there are higher beings who, like us, are working with individuals such as Trydjya to accelerate their process, so that they can fulfil their missions and serve the greater whole. Others are joining together under the guidance of dedicated shamans and sensitives, whose purpose it is to draw consciousness into these vortices as part of individual and planetary initiation. However, unless they join hands with the Earth Keepers of those sacred centres, they will be unable to unlock the secrets contained there, no matter how pure their intentions nor how sincere their promises of mystical experiences and spiritual awakenings.

Whatever your experience, whatever you bring back into your world from your migrations and soul journeys, it is important to remember that you are carrying your vibrations into the sacred sites of Gaia; your soul music, the *wam*, will be encoded there — forever imprinted in the ethers. Your thoughts and their projections too, become one with the energies of these most powerful Spirit centres, and you have a responsibility to those who have come before you as well as to those who will come after. If you wish to honour Gaia and all life in this, your world, and others yet unknown, you must purify your vibrations, letting go of all feelings of separation and egocentricity before you congregate at the altars. Then, in your humility and honour, will you know the expansion in your hearts and the joy of belonging — beings all in the greatness of the One.

Sites of worship are pulsating with the energies of angelic beings, elemental spirits, interplanetary council, many initiates, adepts and masters, and you will feel the power of group soul when you join together in worship. You can feel the spirits of the light congregating, focusing consciousness at the sites. This is part of your attraction there, for as you dance across the junctures in the starlight days of great transformation you are weaving the Gossamer Web, reuniting with the Mother. Hasten, for you must accomplish a great deal from now until the closing of time, and by taking yourselves to her power you are committing your conscious acknowledgement of Gaia, while fusing with other light beings who, like you, are coming home — speeding up your process by leaps and bounds.

The nine centres of Earth's primary energy network are: the Giza Plateau, Mt Kailas in Tibet, the English Triangulation (Avebury — Glastonbury — Stonehenge), Brittany, the Peruvian Andes, Mt Shasta in California, the Pyramid Valley of Tenochtitlan in Mexico, Oahu in Hawaii and the Native American energy wheels of New Mexico. The secondary sites include Ayers Rock in Australia, Damascus in Syria, certain vortex areas in Siberia (still to be investigated), Mt Sinai in Israel, Easter Island, and Native American energy wheels in Mexico, Guatemala and the United States. You must travel far, overcoming many obstacles, but that is the nature of initiation and most of you, the awakening, have already set off upon your journeys. The time is upon you and there is no turning back so, go now, and spread the light.

Our instrument has stood between the arms of the Great

Sphinx in the cool hours of full moon at Giza, embraced in the violet rays of Gaia's sleep, and has heard the music through the multidimensional portal, the heartbeat and the pulse of the Earth Mother. In light body, she has crossed the threshold of the marble stele and retrieved the memory of other incarnations in Egypt, while leaving her imprint in the ethers. Alone, she has entered the Great Octahedron of Giza in the pre-dawn hours of its silent majesty and lain in the granite chariot, for it is from there that we guided her on her ecstatic voyage through the portal. Facilitated by yet another star woman, Trydjya has crawled on hands and knees into the deep underground chamber to board the great ships of other kingdoms, where she reigned sovereign in ancient days ... recollections of her responsibilities, her mission, her gifts. Every moment of exploration, of remembering, has served to increase her receptivity and attune her mind, so that she would be capable of receiving and deciphering these transmissions, while retrieving the most relevant bits and pieces of her ancient history of incarnations on this and other planes.

Her journeys through the vast lands of Tibet have served to rekindle Atlantean memory of sound upon form, so that she could receive and decipher the complexity of our message, for in order to activate the channel, Trydjya had to feel the Wisdom in her heart. In Burma, we reunited her with her former Master, the Holy One, Uarditt Sa, who walked with her in the time of her incarnation as *Tse Den*, the boy Lama of Kumbum Temple. From that meeting she has known a most powerful initiation with the opening of the third eye. In her many voyages through the Orient she was shown the road of the middle way, rekindling within her soul the know-ledge of the Buddhist path to enlightenment. But it was not until her crop circle visitations, first in the Hyperdimensional Spiral at Stonehenge Temple and later in the Fractal Triangulation near Silbury Hill,[1] that we were able to establish clear channel link-up, for then communication was unfettered and instantaneous. There, as she lay for the first time in the crop glyph, encircled in the light of sacred Sirian form and morphology, Trydjya was cleared to receive us: a collective consciousness — Speakers of the High Council.

The Julia Set. This magnificent crop circle appeared next to Stonehenge in July 1996.

Those of you who have yet to explore the circle glyphs will, in these next few Earth years, find yourselves drawn in greater numbers to the fields of England. There you will discover the most significant signs of stellar consciousness currently manifesting in your dimension. This is contact, an answer to the call of SETI,[2] a response to the rudimentary images your leading space organisation (NASA) has been emitting out into the Cosmos for years, seeking a reply — some sign of intelligent life in the universe.

Do you fully realise that the 'top secret' committees of your military leadership never intended that greetings from your brothers and sisters of the galaxy should be shared with the people of your world? Once again, the Power wishes to dissuade you, to hold back the information for their own military and economic interests and so you are made to feel ludicrous and immature if you dare to recognise the truths which lie coded in the flattened stalks of wheat. For, what would happen if you, an entire populace, suddenly became aware that intelligent extraplanetary beings from within your galaxy have been working with your governments for years? Or that free energy is available on Earth, or that the entire arsenal of nuclear weapons currently threatening annihilation of life on Gaia could be disbanded instantaneously?

Wouldn't the power structure fall immediately? Wouldn't Wall Street crash, as values shifted away from the current strongholds — the resources that are being stripped from the Earth's very core? Wouldn't war, product of your being stimulated into feelings of separation and subdivided into contrasting religions, countries, races and beliefs, cease, with the knowledge that you are the Earth people, inhabitants of the garden of Eden, one of many species of intelligent beings populating the material universe? Indeed, wouldn't your focus be altered entirely as you scanned the Cosmos to meet the long awaited parentage of your ancestral families?

If we are evoking feelings of defensive resistance within you, thoughts that the scenario is too diabolical for even you to believe, then we ask you to consider why the mass of humanity has only remotely heard of the crop circles: and why the majority has been led by media propaganda to believe that they are the mad fantasy of a couple of drooling old fools who had nothing better to do than to drag a plank through crop for what would have to have been excruciatingly long hours ... trudging around in circles in the dark nights of their ennui. But why? Even if there were a remote possibility that these simple men could truly have been the architects of such profound forms, what possible motivation might they have had to warrant such arduous endeavour?

'Putting the world on for a laugh' was declared to be the driving motivation behind the phenomenon — a bit of mischievous fun. As hypotheses go, that might explain a few misshapen rounds of flattened crop, but certainly carries no credibility when one gazes upon the symmetry and geometric design of the intricate glyphs. Neither does it account for the sheer numbers of formations that have been laid over the years. For since many summers past have we been recreating our works of galactic design and symbolism in the fields, bringing you more complexity of form and raising the sound and light frequencies within them. Where are the media reports of the human interest variety — stories of the incredible transformational experiences many people have undergone upon witnessing and entering into the circles?

Royal Air Force helicopters are frequently seen hovering over the glyphs, and it is quite common to the explorers of the circles to witness Air Force personnel filming overhead, zooming in to the activity in the fields. Some of you realise that they are actually spying on the visitors to the circles … keeping files on just who is bringing the information to the mainstream. Trydjya, in fact, has been photographed lying in the central vortex circle of the Hyperdimensional Spiral, receiving attunement. There is much humour in that invasion of her liberty, for they are going through the motions, but don't know what it is they are looking for. There are countless witnesses who have given their personal testimony of Air Force helicopters over the glyphs. Surely the military wouldn't be wasting taxpayers' money just to follow up on some insignificant pranksters, would they? Given your resistance to unjust and obsessive taxation, we must deduce that you would rebel against such inane waste. What, then, do you suppose, is their true interest in the crop circle phenomenon?

Credible members of your scientific and spiritual communities have been identifying within the glyphs' complex composition equations, multidimensional geometry, fractal mathematics, and biogeometrical form and vibration. Still, we observe with curiosity, the population *en masse* is willing to accept the establishment explanation of what is perhaps the most tangible manifestation of interdimensional communication occurring now on your planet: first, that two elderly, fun-seeking pranksters possess such a wealth of information; and second, that they could have the capability to express that wisdom in such perfect forms as those you are now witnessing across the English countryside.

The establishment wants you to ignore the messages laid into the crops, denying that their complex and meaningful geometric configurations are actual representations of intelligent life of other realms and refusing you your place in the cosmic scheme of things. This is why you would be wise to experience the crop circles firsthand — for your own edification — for if we are imprinting Sirian symbols into your third-dimensional fields of vision, it is to communicate with you — to stimulate you into response. We are bringing you the proof, a tangible message, something that you can believe is real. Ours is a desire to shake the population out of its narcotic trance — its sedation — to help the unaware become conscious of all that surrounds them. However, you will have to first open your eyes to what is visible in your reality, before you will be able to see what is hovering around you in the ethers.

It is quite revealing to those outside of your experience that the indisputable clarity of the glyphs, their extradimensional origins, has impacted only a very limited group of individuals. This is a reflection of just how blind the masses are in their perception of what surrounds them. Anaesthetised, they stare into the holographic machines filling their bodies with the drug of indifference, and from their armchairs of inertia and addiction, condemn you for your brilliance and perception — your daring to question authority or doubt convention. Soon they will be faced with the karmic consequence of that indifference for, unless they open to change, they will not have developed consciousness to integrate the higher energies and shifting time. Many will opt to leave, to reincarnate in other worlds where they can continue their evolutionary process at a much slower pace ... and that is as it should be. Those of you who will remain, however, must be roused from your sleep so that you can unite your efforts to bring Gaia back to balance before the final phase of her transition.

Universal law requires that all sentient beings honour the free will of every other living being, and is therefore designed as a model of non-interventionism: that is, guidance is to be given freely to the seeker and never to be imposed upon those who do not ask for it. To do so would be to interfere with their karma and would move against natural process. However, as a race you have an obligation to Gaia, to the children and to those life forms that are unable to communicate ... unable to ask for help. We are therefore free to warn you of the dangers that you face as beings on a planet which is experiencing the acceleration of brutality and plundering of yet unawakened beings who simply cannot perceive what lies ahead for Planet Earth and all of humanity. The signs are all around you; they are increasingly alarming and are manifesting at all points of the globe. The winds have begun to blow. And just as only a very select few of you are willing to recognise the cosmic wisdom in the fields of England, so only a small minority of the global population reads the signs a dying Earth is sending to her keepers, as she struggles to survive the relentless hand of man.

It is our observation that of those small but growing numbers of you who have experienced the crop circles, the clairsencient need but approach their perimeters to feel the currents running through the glyphs and into their bodies; the clairvoyant can actually see energy forms and light beings there; the clairaudient, such as Trydjya, have lain in the glyphs, attuned the *wam* to the altered frequencies and made the galactic connection — the channels cleared for direct transmission from Sirian Council. Others are simply awed by their beauty and complexity of form, and many are the profound revelations of those of you who have been called. Whatever your personal response to a crop glyph, you can rest assured that entering a circle brings you into our resonant fields, altering your DNA and raising your vibration to facilitate your expanding energy fields.

Despite establishment attempts to distract and distance you from the formations, greater numbers will be drawn to the fields to witness and experience firsthand the indisputable demonstration of higher knowledge, which we continue to imprint upon the earth of Gaia. Each glyph carries the data, codes and information of the Sirian Keys to Universal Ascension, for these are our works — our preferred milieu of sound upon form and sacred symbolism — the light of consciousness made manifest.

We are well aware of your burning desire to know just how the crop circles are formed and we are delighted by your many theories, profound intuitions and scientific investigations. It is a moving experience watching humanity stretching and reaching with your minds. We delight as you open your hearts, like wondrous children, to your galactic family. As you lie quietly in the fields of wheat, nurtured by the cosmic energies flowing through you, feeling the love and the wonder of belonging, we savour your reverence and amazement. The connection fills us with joy and celebration. Those of you who have already entered, **know** … for your Spirit has been inexorably altered from that moment on and you radiate with the excitement of your experience … the sense of belonging. Reunion. You, the awakening ones, can feel what's coming. You are pulsating to the beat of the galactic dance, and we connect to your rhythm just as you beat to ours. It is exchange, memory and anticipation. It is the heartsong: the Music of the Spheres.

The technical explanation of how the glyphs are imposed upon the crop is already known to you, buried in the deep memory of your race consciousness. We are simply utilising that forgotten Gaian wisdom which we have described to you in an earlier lesson, in our discussion of the passing of sound frequencies through sacred geometrical forms. Like the Tibetan Priesthood, we employ the use of sound imposed upon sacred symbols to materialise consciousness. The process involves activating the energy grids of those projected landscape areas; synthesising Earth's responsive magnetic field; attuning to the *wam* of Gaia and focusing the consciousness of those highly aware Earth beings who are predisposed to our frequencies. This is all that is required for us to be able to imprint sixth-dimensional consciousness upon your material reality. It appears much more complex in the telling than it is in the doing. We ask that you do not allow yourselves to be overwhelmed by the words, for language must communicate experience and this is yours yet to discover.

This procedure is not much different than projecting flying craft into your vision, and certainly the phenomenon of UFOs in the skies has been perceived by hundreds of thousands of individuals. We can confirm that conscious beings traversing the material universe would require physical spaceships, and these do exist … while higher-dimensional beings transcend the physical. But we do project to you images of disks and mother ships, for that is what you expect of extraterrestrial intelligence while you are still confined in your third-dimensional world. And so, if it is space-ships you want, we can and do create them for you: holographic images that appear to be of the material realm, but are not.

We do not need ships to journey to other worlds, and neither do you. We have spoken of the ancient Egyptians and the Tibetan Lamas, and how they journeyed in body to other dimensions and other realities. However, we are not suggesting that you attempt to re-establish their methodology at this time in your development, for it simply is not necessary. We have told you in many ways … the knowledge is within you and has always been coded there, in your DNA, awaiting retrieval — the turning of the keys.

You have vast storehouses of knowledge to pull up into con-scious awareness at this moment, and so we are pleased to see that you are getting over your UFO fascination — moving beyond it — for it is distracting you from the bigger picture. Besides, for over forty years the Secret Government has been working with alien scientists to produce some of the more rudimentary space-craft flying through space, and much of what you are observing in your skies is merely the product of their advanced engineering.

Spinning disk technology, as we mentioned earlier, involves altering levels of gravitational force and releasing matter from the pull of gravity. This knowledge is fundamental to unrestricted travel through the material universe, a necessary technology for extensive penetration into the depths of space. However, much of humanity is moving beyond the material planes now, readjusting your focus to new possibilities and much greater horizons.

While your covert military agencies gloat over their acquisition of the 'secret technology', to intelligent life in the galaxy it is common knowledge, for there is enormous commerce and cultural exchange throughout the Cosmos, and interplanetary travel benefits all peaceful civilisations. The irony of it all — their coveting of the knowledge and the secrecy surrounding their experimentation with spinning disks — is that by the time they get around to openly admitting their capabilities to the people of Earth, your planet will be in such an altered state of consciousness that, as a race, you will have moved way past caring.

Note

1. The Hyperdimensional Spiral at Stonehenge Temple refers to the Julia Set (see photo), laid down across the road from Stonehenge in July 1996. The Fractal Triangulation near Silbury Hill refers to the Fractal Star of David laid in a field below Silbury Hill in July 1997.

2. SETI (Search for Extraterrestrial Intelligence): NASA's project involving the sending of sound patterns into space in hopes of receiving an intelligent response.

Ten

THE ONE CODED MASTER

———————————

The One Coded Master, still imperceptible to most of your world, enters mass mind only when enough of you are cleared to hold her vibrational pattern at your frequency — which we can tell you begins to occur in your Earth year 2010. This is not the 'Messiah', nor is it our intention to present her as your saviour, so please do not give your power away to that possibility, for it would mean that you have completely misinterpreted our message. Those of you who have begun the work of clearing your fields and moving out of fear have realised that you are being pointed in the right direction, guided by your higher consciousness, and that nothing outside of you is going to be able to do that for you.

It is your focus and purity of intent that will lead you through the desert of the Gaian winter; it will be your feelings of community, your sense of the whole, that will bring the planet through the starless night. Dreams of the Messiah and other saviours can be relinquished now, yielding to the inner knowing (your strength and sense of purpose) with which each of you holds your own frequency, taking responsibility for all thoughts that you send across the waves; taking responsibility for every deed, every act, every word.

The bodyworkers are available now to assist you in the shifting and clearing of the energies, and the true teachers are bringing through the message. Have you felt the scintillating waves of light moving through you? Surely you are stunned by the acceleration being experienced on so many levels, for never before has your family of celestial bodies known such vibrational intensity, and every planet of your solar system, in turn, has begun its metamorphosis. All is interrelated, all is experienced in every living creature of your Solar Deity, from the far reaches of the outer orbits to the innermost spheres and there, within the explosive mass of the gaseous star — your central Sun.

Entering into the foreground now are revolutionary new thinkers in the fields of astronomy and astrology, those who will be clear to chart the new byways, for the relationships of the heavenly bodies will soon take on altered proportions as the planets begin their acute stages of transmutation, and the old paradigms will no longer fit. The archetypes are blossoming into more complex personae, and new bodies are emerging from the obscurity of the unexplored. As your Sun begins its collapse, all is pulled inward, and the yet undiscovered will come into the light and then move through the vortex with you.

There are the new leaders, strong icons in whom you can place your trust, those who will guide you through the cataclysms of the tearing realities and bring you to the calm. There are the mothers and the healing teams to nurture and restore the energies; seers and gifted instruments to bring through the Wisdom. Others will serve as record keepers — those who will carry the genetic codes into the next dimension. There are the Earth Keepers, who will hold Gaian vibration and facilitate your activation when you take yourselves to the sites. But do not delude yourselves with imaginings of a great saviour, for that is simply a mythical allegory. As light beings, you will join together and within the sacred circles of your union will you find protection and safe harbour in your love of Gaia and all that is pulsating to the heartbeat of the universe.

When earlier we introduced the One Coded Master as one whose mission it is to help lead you back into the light, we did not mean to imply that she is a physical being, although there are many who would be ecstatic to claim title. For this reason, we will make only such reference to her as is necessary to fulfil our purpose in these transmissions, which is: to initiate perception of her presence in this difficult stage of your planetary evolution, and to extend that awareness to as many human beings as is possible, so that you can receive her in your hearts and accept her into group mind.

When we speak of the Coded One, we refer to an Ascended Master who has served at many intervals of consciousness throughout Universal Being. She comes into your realm as a sort of galactic midwife to assist in your Solar Deity's rebirthing. She has already descended from beyond the Andromedan Galaxy, the tenth dimension, in preparation of what will be required of her — the monumental task of setting the lock-on points of the celestial bodies of your Solar Deity. This requires conscious mind powers so beyond our capabilities that we are somewhat awestricken by its magnitude ... for here we are speaking of one entity affecting the course of an entire solar system as it slips out of one dimensional context into another.

This is an unimaginable assignment, even from our perspective, so that to attempt description is futile at this point in our common development. We can tell you, however, that she enters to unlock the portals of every celestial body in your solar system and to set the interplanetary gravitational linkage for the journey through the great vortex of Universal Being's astral chords, which takes place when the proper galactic alignments and planetary conjunctions coincide with the Mayan coordinates. This involves parallel universes, multidimensional celestial beings, and your beloved solar family of planets, moons and asteroids, which will all have moved into optimum position at the Mayan projection point of 21 December, 2012.

Of the descent of the Coded Master, we do not wish to imply that she takes human form or crystallises as matter; indeed, a vibrational essence of this intensity cannot be condensed into a physical body. Let us just say that that would be like trying to hold a quart of pure uranium in a plastic bottle. Her essence already permeates your atmosphere, particularly concentrated over the vortexes, for it is from the Earth realm that she will coordinate the planetary linkage.

As you will not experience the Coded One as a physical deity, we advise you to be wary of those who will claim to witness her image in the abstract forms of clouds and the trees. She is beyond form, a being of such vibrational magnitude that there can be no specific visual reference, nor spoken word. She is essence, consciousness of the purest intensity, performing a mission ... assisting in the rebirthing of a Deity.

Some of you have begun to connect with her at the primary energy level, the first in increasingly intense stages of communication that may be reached via a step-up process of alignments — so great is her light. The presence enters your awareness as a most intense brilliance, a radiant iridescence that is non-existent in your present spectrum, but rest assured that you will know it when it moves through you.

More will become aware of her presence in the first days of the new millennium and it will be that very brilliance that will spark your awareness, a sign that you have reached Level One acclimatisation. This is colour that you will feel deep within you, which moves in to create the necessary alterations at the subatomic level ... just as at other moments in your evolution have you absorbed frequencies from other dimensions that have brought you into resonance. The radiance of the Coded Master enters into the subatomic make-up of every being on the planet and beyond, throughout your Solar Deity's body, the exhilarating prelude to your final passage into the next level.

If it is now, through these teachings, that you are being introduced to this entity, then you are initiating at this moment your conscious perception of her — a preliminary to receiving the vibrational adjustments, which will begin once you simply allow yourselves to hold the probability of such a being in your conscious thoughts. This is not going to be readily accepted by your rational minds, for it is still quite inconceivable to you that a being of such magnitude could exist. Here we are describing an Ascended Master resonating as a Deity, and we know how very difficult it is for western culture, still enslaved by your white male-dominant religions, to embrace the Goddess.

All beings, in the process of their ascension along the spiral, become more God-like. We ask that you consider that statement a spiritual given. Just as you move through karma as it manifests in your physical lifetimes, so do you, as spirit beings, evolve eventually into that uncontainable light vibration of the luminary

— the evolved soul. Long is the journey to initiation, further yet to mastery and beyond ... to ascension; it is the same path for all souls ... the road home to Supreme Being. All creation is in that state of upward mobility of becoming and returning to Source. The One Coded Master has reached that point of merging, but she must first consecrate this final act as individual consciousness: her contribution to the Great Work of alchemy; a process of healings and gravitational alignments that will bring your Solar Deity through the tunnel, and in passing, the entire system turns to gold.

Our instrument, Trydjya, is at this time being prepared for the Level Three acclimatisation, which will bring her into greater synergy with the reverberations of the Master's energy. This, in turn, will further facilitate her interaction with this Council and beings of yet higher dimensions, who will begin communication with Earth in the very near future. This is part of the continuous process of attunement necessary for her future work as the instrument of our collective voice and orator of the Desert Days.

The One Coded Master enters to define the proper alignments required to assure safe transit, re-establishing within the Solar Deity's body the sound frequencies that will help hold your solar system together, just as the Dolphin Beings have carried your seas. She holds the codes of all the key vortex points of every celestial body in your solar system, and her mission is to clear the energy meridians of Solar Deity; establish the correct gravitational linkage between the force fields of all the bodies; and, in a sense, direct the orchestra of this final symphony.

We understand that without her intervention, your solar system would break up, for unless the celestial bodies have been dynamically integrated, the siphoning effect of that magnetic passage could send planets, moons and asteroid clusters slamming into one another in a great galactic collision — or fling them into the outermost quadrants of hyperdimensional space. Others could simply disappear in the grey zone between the dimensions, the least desirable fate for all souls in transition.

The grey zone can be likened to the thickest fog, an impenetrable nebulus between life and death, where the unresolved soul can remain trapped in passing through the transitional phases of the death process … somewhere between matter and spirit. Trust that this is a place you do not want to be, neither as individual units in your own life-death cycles, nor as a celestial body in transit to its next dimension. It is here that the infamous 'greys', your stereotyped extraterrestrial villains, reside. From these murky vapours they have slipped into manifold frameworks in the material universe, always a disturbance to the harmony of three-dimensional beings. They are neither of the physical nor of the spiritual, and so create much fear and discomfort when making an appearance in your realities. As an aside, we wish to emphasise that these beings are not of the light, and that your growing infatuation with them — the statuettes, T-shirts and other paraphernalia, books and movies — holds them in your conscious awareness. That is unwise, particularly at this sensitive moment, when so much is at stake.

You are so much more insightful when you focus your creative visions of extraplanetary beings on images that bring light into your aura, rather than filling the spaces between you with illusions from the grey world. We know that you understand how thought can and does manifest as you project it into your framework, and this is one reality you truly prefer to leave alone, believe us.

The Coded Master becomes a predominant force during the year 2010, when time enters the extreme phase of its warp, before coming to a complete halt at winter solstice in 2012. You will be faced with many incongruities as linear time begins to close down around you. As bizarre as events appear to you now, you cannot imagine what awaits you once you reach this point on the wheel. You will witness the reappearance of extinct species, multi-dimensional beings bleeding through the layers, specific events of your past reoccurring and the borders of reality simply beginning to burst apart. There will be an infinity of conflicting images, contradictions of every sort, and confusion at this point of the transformation will reign — as beings from all walks of life are faced with the inconsonance of the merging realities.

As the effects of the vibrational shift intensify your emotional, mental and physical bodies, the geological conditions of the Earth are intensifying as well. With the acceleration of time and increasing rips and tears in the time-space construct, you will be forced to confront innumerable 'un-realities'. Many will frantically search for logical explanations, and in your terms will simply lose their minds; others, who have been accelerating their light bodies and evolving out of limitation while holding centre, will recognise the breakdown of the walls of time as expansion beyond the confines of the third dimension, moving through it all at fulcrum point.

Those of you who are able to comprehend and resonate to the powerful vibrational surge that is coming in for you now with the Coded Master are the gifted. You have cleared your energies and have already worked through all residual fear, and so you are actually looking forward to the shift, knowing that it will be glorious: the refinement of polarity, the end of time and freedom from illusion. Her emanations will be a most significant part of your quickening, a source of unconscious inspiration, and you are ready, soaring on the wings of anticipation.

The Coded One is embodied in the effigies of the Egyptian goddess, Hathor, as she is depicted with the solar disk embedded in Her horns — for the Egyptians knew that she held your Solar Deity, *Ra*, in balance. We remind you that all is written in the Akasha, all foreseen in the no-time, and many of the Priesthood of Egypt were gifted seers — guided by the star beings of the Pleiades and Sirius, who walked among them.

She is as Sothis, the dog star of Sirius, ascending symbolically at your dawning, just as in the ancient days of Egypt when the rising of Sothis on the Eastern horizon, before the dawn, was always a precursor to the flooding of the Nile, which brought fertility and life to the arid lands of the Egyptian Valley. Unfortunately, the flood waters of the new millennium cannot be compared to the cyclical swelling of the Nile Valley, the great lifeline of Egypt, for what you have begun to experience as raging waters and angry seas in these, your days, are only the beginning of nature's unleashing fury ... Gaia's response to the imbalance and disharmony that has resulted from your indifference and neglect.

You have been warned and forewarned of the Earth Changes that have already begun to manifest furiously across the globe, and it is not our purpose to constantly beat you with reports of the crises now facing your planet. We cannot emphasise enough, however, that you possess the power to alter the current projections of a devastating, violent transition for Gaia — even though the signs and prophecies tend to deny you a positive outcome.

It is not too late to initiate resolution. This is the crucial play; the checkmate moment lies before you. However, returning to our observation of 'eyes that will not see', we question whether you, the race, will move in time to win the game, reversing the effects of your errors and establishing a new paradigm for fourth-dimensional Earth.

In her transition to the higher dimension, Gaia does undergo a natural planetary death, for that is the nature of transition. If you find this concept upsetting, it is because you are still fearful of the unknown wonder of passage out of the physical realm. Remember, however, that you are familiar with death, for most of you have made the personal transition many hundreds of times before. The information is there, as we repeat again and again, in your genetic material — buried in the subconscious pool.

Gaia's current ecological crisis is an unnatural prelude to her transmutation, a symptom of humanity's separation from nature and the Earth. You are exacerbating the process of her transition with your all-out destruction of the ecosystems, it does not have to play out that way. Just like the human experience of death, there can be a sweet, gentle passing. Your own karma and the individual approach to the health of the body determines whether your personal transition blows like a gentle wind or a violent storm. So it is with Gaia, whose disease and unwellness are the products of your community unconsciousness. Just as you have all contributed to her suffering, you can all unite forces to heal her, preparing for the final phase of her transition.

Large factions of your population and the majority of the establishment, still in denial, adamantly refuse to accept that an ecological crisis even exists. This, as we observe the smoke rising above the burning timbers of your dying rainforests, and the tentacles of black crude reaching across your seas, will render the passage a most painful journey. It is a sobering experience, observing Earth from our viewing post, for Gaia was once one of the most breathtaking habitats in the universe ... paradise and beauty of unparalleled measure. And such music! Her *wam* sang out into the heavens, like the sirens to Ulysses, and many were the voyagers of space lured into Earth's atmosphere in those ancient days of your harmonious coexistence with the elemental energies. Man knew his place amongst the living, and humbled himself before the unseen forces of the universe, the primordial gods and the animals.

All was in balance and love prevailed; all was harmonious in the Garden of Eden.

We have observed your governmental leaders at work in the Kyoto Summit, where they recently met to discuss global warming. They resolved to reduce by a token eight per cent their toxic emissions by your year 2008: far too little, much too late. In this scenario, industry wins, Gaia loses, and so do you. You have seen the beginnings of the drifting apart of Antarctica (the last of the unspoilt ecosystems) and by the time your governments honour their commitments to enact the inadequate reduction plans promised in

1998, many of your cities and coastal regions will be under water; the entire glacial mass will have cracked apart, with large islands moving up against portions of South America and melting in the warmer waters.

Know that this is not mere prophecy we are speaking of here. It is already happening — it was already a manifesting reality in 1998. In the event that you happened to miss this 'Earth-shattering' news during its brief appearance in your media, a huge island of ice detached from the pole and began its migration towards the warmer waters off the southernmost tip of Argentina.

This one event alone will be the cause of great floods, as we are talking about an entire island of ice slowly melting in those waters, and other glaciers and ice walls are breaking off all the time. You can look forward to an extension of the *El Niño* phenomenon, no longer the sporadic exception, which is a direct result of global warming, as is the dissolution of Antarctica. Massive flooding is already occurring in many areas of the world, but until now you have yet to know real fury. The rising water levels, combined with your suffocation of the soil of Gaia with cement and concrete, will cause unbelievable devastation. Much of your current shorelines will be redefined, while many coastal cities and towns will actually disappear forever, engulfed by the rising tides, flood waters and raging rivers. Surely you have begun to sense that many will be migrating to safer areas in the upcoming years, forced out of their homes and communities in search of dry land and higher ground.

You have another pressing issue resulting from the flooding crisis, as it is already being experienced at this time. As the flood waters of your oceans and rivers rampage across your farmlands and fertile fields, they are destroying much of your food supply and poisoning more. Waste and debris are swept along in the raging waters, and as they recede you find the land is saturated with the filth of human waste and toxic garbage swept along in the deluge, contaminating the soil for many, many years into the future.

Gaia cannot wait until 2008 for the insignificant eight per cent reduction, nor can you, as breathing beings on the planet. You will need to congregate and unite forces to persuade and direct your world leaders to address the ecological breakdown of Earth with great urgency, for although the puppeteers are directing them to focus attention on international relations, the arms race, global economy and the advancement of technology, we are telling you that there is no more pressing concern currently facing humanity than that of the environment.

Ecology must move to the forefront of your awareness and become the primary concern of every being on the planet. Governments can be pressured into response, and those industries which insist upon choking the life out of Gaia can be monitored and finally brought to a halt. You are the consumers; you control industry through your purchasing power, for the money god sets the stage in your global policies. If you simply refuse products that do not conform to rigid environmental regulations, as well as rejecting those that create disease within you (such as the irradiated produce that is now appearing on your shelves), government will have no choice but to create the legislation that you, the people, demand. As a consequence, industry will be forced to either meet the standards and the requirements of the population, or shut down their operations. Either of these two options is a positive solution to the problem of industry's free reign over the Earth. For the rest, you will have to sacrifice, perhaps be inconvenienced and occasionally spend more for products that are environmentally safe. Industry's argument is that implementing ecological standards is simply not cost efficient — but it could be if you, as a people, would move as a buying force to those environment-friendly products and away from the others. Do you understand the power of your unity, and why you are manoeuvred into separation?

Where are you, children of Gaia? Are you prepared to use your will, to join as a collective consciousness, and come to the rescue of the Great Mother? By uniting forces with those who have the courage to risk their personal security for the good of the Earth, you can move mountains. What has happened to your ability to discern what is just for your planet? You must have the courage to stand for your beliefs, to go against the grain if it means honouring Truth. When will you insist upon solutions, enact legislation and do your part to heal the planet, while you can still effect change? What of the animals, the great birds and the fish? Do you realise they are slowly disappearing from the face of the planet? What will it take before you move beyond your resignation and fight back, uniting forces to protect and save your land, seas and the very air you breathe?

The authorities — the primary decision makers — still do not hear your voice, for it is too soft, too weak. We are calling upon you to go into the masses and pull people up to the knowledge, so that your sheer numbers will raise the volume — so that they will be forced to listen. It is not enough to be outraged at the crimes being committed against the Earth Mother; you have to contribute to the community to effect change. Your united front is vitality, the moving force, and so is your individual commitment to reducing consumption, careful and correct elimination of waste and overall conscious behaviour as it contributes to the harmonious rebalancing of Gaia.

Our warnings will end soon, for it will be too late and there will be no way back if you do not heed the message and take decisive action. It is up to you now. Take command out of love for your planet and for all the magnificence of life it has known throughout its immeasurable history. And do not forget that you will still be Earth-centred in the new dimension; that is, the Earth moves through, and you with her ... for you are the beings of Gaia. So, if you are thinking in terms of a Disneyland happy ending where, regardless, all is rectified in the new, remember that karma must resolve, and Gaia's ills will be just as real in the fourth dimension even though the ascension process will have altered their manifestation.

You are learning that only through the resolution of your karmic debts can you free yourselves, and it is the same for your planet. We wish to provide you with food for thought as to just what the fourth-dimensional reality might hold for Gaia if you don't get to work immediately — for you are about to enter the irreversible phase when all is pulled into the vortex faster than the speed of light.

The One Coded Master has no jurisdiction over the matter of the health and balance of Earth's ecosystems, for that is a karmic responsibility that must be resolved through your race consciousness. It is linked to the whole, and therefore it is an aspect of her healing function, but do not believe that a saviour arrives at the brink and delivers the world from calamity, for this is victim consciousness — the antithesis of what is required of you now.

We can tell you that Gaia is currently the most unstable celestial body in your solar system, and is for many reasons considered the weak link of the Solar Deity. Paradoxically, it is also the most dynamic, for the potential of human consciousness is vast and inexhaustible and we witness from the reading of the Akashic Record that the beings of Earth are capable of unfathomable works of love and compassion — particularly at the pinnacles of crisis. Your great capacity to feel intense emotion, after all, is a very vital aspect of your humanity, and we encourage you to know your emotional bodies in their complexity. We are fascinated by your emotionalism, for when you are filled with love, you are capable of experiencing extreme joy, pleasure and the ecstasy of life — it is a delight to experience those waves rolling through our realms. We are grateful to you. Your emotions, when exalted by love, are a most powerful aspect of your humanity, which moves you to greatness. Your rapture is felt throughout the heavens.

This is one of the primary reasons why so much attention has been focused upon you ... why so many eyes are watching, and why the One Coded Master has decided to operate her great work from your planetary field.

Eleven

THE SECRET GOVERNMENT AND
THE SPACE CONSPIRACY

We observe your military at work in the Cosmos and the covert activities of their space programmes. We believe it is time that you, the people, learn about what is being perpetrated in space so that you can act upon the information and solicit from your governments the truth of their discoveries. What they are unearthing as your representatives must benefit all of humanity, rather than serve only those of the Power: the human élite — the Secret Government. You have every right, as citizens of the world and members of the galactic family, to **know**. To accelerate the process of your awakening, your liberation out of control and manipulation, you need information, for knowledge is light.

We wish to tell you that official statements regarding your government's probing of space, or contact with other species, or the developments on your Moon and the red planet are quite different from what we are watching from our vantage point. Given that space exploration is beyond your personal experience at this moment, you remain almost entirely dependent upon government for all information of space and your expansion into the heavens, and their data are considered the scientific fruit of your progress — a sort of pictorial Bible of all that which humanity knows to exist beyond Planet Earth.

But there is another version, the multidimensional viewpoint, which we believe you are entitled to hear as well, after which you can decide for yourselves, with alert mind and conscious soul, which of the two accounts of human penetration of space rings true to you at a very deep, intuitional level … there where the logical mind can also be appeased and find harbour. It is so that we intend to share our observations of your spacemen at work in the Cosmos and divulge to you the secrets of their acquired knowledge. You may be sceptical, and that is understandable, for what we offer here denies loyalties to government, to the ideals of the *Patria* and to existing belief systems. Yet, we ask that you open yourselves to the possibility of a different message from that which, until recently, has been driven into you through the vehicle of your media. We ask that you let the information in, savour it, chew it up and then spit out that which leaves the worst taste in your mouths — digesting the rest.

Fortunately, there are brave new pioneers who are openly asking questions and demanding answers, brilliant ones who dare to confront the Power. Their insistence is now shaking the scientific communities and forcing recognition — pressuring the offending military leaders to divulge more regarding the true goings-on in the space conspiracy. They are those of the scientific orientation, whose works regarding the true purpose of current military and scientific exploration of the Moon and the Martian landscape are absolutely illuminating. Because of their creative insights, determination and persistence, you are finally getting to some of the truth regarding extraterrestrial life as it appears to have existed on other planets in linear constructs of past and future, but which, you are learning, is all part of the no-time of existence.

We observe the pioneer, Richard Hoagland, probing the evidence of NASA's undeclared discoveries in space, and he brings to you the first pieces of hard evidence that life has existed on the red planet and on the Moon. You, seekers of knowledge, are drawing upon this information to fill in the empty spaces of your galactic memory, while searching for the true missing link. Indeed, most of your NASA officials would like to keep all information classified to avoid opening that Pandora's box — your stimulated curiosity. But it is too late, for the Adept Hoagland has shown you the Martian Sphinx and the pyramidal complex of Cydonia and he is piecing together the dome-like structural remnants of ancient cities on the Moon. You simply cannot ignore the undeniable.

Those structures, the remnants discovered in the Adept Hoagland's investigation into the fragments and shards of what was once the glassy dome of a remote civilisation, are the remains of an ancient Annunaki military installation, whose ancient bases of operation lie hidden in the dust-covered artifacts of Luna.

You now have the long-awaited proofs, even though those in command are telling you that these are illusions. Do you join us in defining such explanations paradoxical? It is **from** illusion that you are escaping when you confront the black and white reality of NASA's own imaging of the Martian topography. Don't you consider it an offence to your intelligence that you are boldly denied acknowledgement of the Cydonia images? You are being told by the establishment that you simply do not see what you see; in other words, even proof, that tangible stuff upon which your belief systems claim to be based, is denied you by the authorities, and what you clearly see from their own official photographs they tell you is not there.

Despite attempts to keep the brilliant Richard Hoagland at bay by first denying the images of the Sphinx and then so declaring them 'optical illusions', the Top Secret committees have failed in their policy of absolute secrecy regarding the Martian monuments. His scientific method and astute intuition have combined to bring to you a most convincing, well-documented argument that intelligent life has existed on that planet and left evidence of a highly developed civilisation which finds many parallels on Earth. His theories regarding prior colonisation of the Moon are also valid, but there is much more to uncover there. Much less visible evidence remains on that surface and multidimensional constructs are involved, making it more difficult to penetrate that reality and retrieve the necessary images and information.

To those who censor and condemn the work of men such as the Adept Hoagland, as well as to the critics of those who, like our instrument, Trydjya, are bringing through channelled messages of galactic intelligence, we ask you to remember that only a brief six hundred years ago, the Master Galileo was condemned a heretic for introducing to humanity the concept of the Earth as a spinning globe rotating around a central sun, rather than that which it was believed to be at the time: a two-dimensional, finite surface from which one could fall into the dark abyss of nothingness. For daring to challenge the dogma of church and state, this light one was condemned to the dark galleys of prison, which sent a solemn message to the people: that the challenging of established thought and, therefore, the Authority, would not be tolerated and that to do so would incur a punishment so great that no ideal or pursuit of knowledge was worth the personal sacrifice.

Had only Galileo been encouraged to expand upon his discoveries, to bring into the consciousness of those times the intuitions and higher knowledge that sourced his vision, your 20th Century civilisation would have evolved to such an extent that by now you would already be enjoying commercial inter-planetary travel, much as you currently fly to distant lands of your world as explorers and vacationing travellers. Trust that learning to journey through space is no greater a leap in your technological advancement than was acquiring the aerodynamic knowledge and ability to fly your great craft across the airways of Earth.

As history plays out, the justly named 'Dark Ages' of religious fanaticism and tyranny constitute one of the most destructive periods of all humanity. The suppression of wisdom, freedom and love was burned into your planet's karma and is, to this day, still unresolved. For this reason do we return to the leitmotif of control vs. freedom, for we wish to assist you in raising the emotional frequency of Gaia, so that you can resolve the karmic patterns of your lowest vibrations as beings on Earth and release her from the karmic debt held in those imprinted memories.

Although you believe yourselves to be free men and women now, in what you label the 21st Century, not that much has really changed since the sunless hour of the Master Galileo's internment. The daring ones, explorers of the unknown territories of mind and matter, are often marginalised, ridiculed and ostracised from the mainstream. Those who move too far from the paradigms of conventional thought, or call you to rebellion against the master … those who dare to expose the Power and question authority, are

dealt with in various unsavoury ways. Some 'disappear'; others are
silenced through fear of reprisal; but the majority of those who go
against the grain are simply condemned as modern day heretics,
eccentric oddities who don't fit into the mainstream and whose
theories are often dismissed as fantasy and fiction. They are pub-
licly challenged and every attempt is made to render their ideas
untenable, so that by the time the public is actually confronted
with their works, they have lost their credibility and impact,
watered down in the ambiguity of your manipulated emotional
denial. Fortunately, you are awakening in growing numbers and,
in seeking out the light of knowledge, you are now creating the
harmonic vibration necessary to override the status quo and
anchor the new energies. The teachers are coming forward, and
you are listening.

Moreover, you are **hearing**.

Nonetheless, the politics of mind control, as in the Atlantean
days of absolute domination, as in the terror-filled hours of the
Dark Ages, still continues. It is the method that has changed, for in
these, your modern times, most of you truly believe that you are
free beings, protected by the fundamental precepts of democracy:
government 'by the people'. This socio-economic structure has
positioned itself as the pole of communism, and its very foundation
depends upon your belief in free speech, free thought and the
other illusory canons of your Independence Declarations.
However, while you are lulled into complacency with your vision
of being a free people, you are subtly manoeuvred and exploited,
treated as mass mind. You are subliminally controlled through
advertising, programming, inaudible sound frequencies and many
more covert technologies that assure the Authority your predetermined emotional reactions. We have told you. The Power looks
upon you as a body of mindless sheep, to be led through the
valley of possibilities to the safe lands of imposed thought, where
you are guided to refuse and ridicule that which exists beyond the
confines of convention, and to honour and defend all that falls
under the umbrella of the dogma — as if those principles are your
own; as if your very identity depends upon upholding them.

It is fascinating to those outside of your realm to observe how you, the awakening, are opening to the reality of life beyond the limits: how you are beginning to embrace the most controversial theories of your existence, even if the masses are still clinging to convention out of fear of the unknown — fear, you must understand, that is deliberately triggered within them.

When you fear, you turn away; you refuse to look; you bury yourselves in ignorance — that is why you are held in fear as a race. Those of the Power want you to look away, to distract yourselves with inane imaginings, so that they can go about their business free of your scrutiny, your questioning. This is the underlying strategy behind the technology of numbing devices: holographic machines, the Internet and computer games for the children. While you become transfixed by these instruments, hypnotised into mass inertia or distracted through stimulation of your animal selves, they are roaming about the Cosmos. They are busily at work on the Moon's surface and initiating now their preliminary invasions of Mars, where the first missions are dedicated to removing all evidence of the City, so that you will stop pestering them with your absorption over things which they feel do not concern you.

Had it not been for the courageous investigations of the Adept Hoagland, you may never have had the privilege of witnessing the archaeological wonders of Mars, absolute proof of civilisations past and key to your own mysteries at Giza and the Triangulation in England. Before long all traces of those monuments will be eliminated, and he, like others before him, will have had the brilliance of his discoveries cast into the shadows of ridicule and incredulity.

Pay attention.

The work of great humanitarians, seekers of the kind of monumental clues to existence which prepare humanity for its giant leaps, has all too often been discredited, destroyed or buried by those who would hold you back so that they can move ahead in secrecy.

Truly, we ask you, is it any wonder that you are having such difficulty getting a handle on the power issue, feeling that you are racing forward without holding the reins? When, as a race, you raise your heads from the drug and start to ask relevant questions or look in the right direction, you are fed doomsday material and propaganda to stimulate your fear mechanisms and to cultivate your doubt and scepticism. You find, in the end, that it is easier just to turn away in a form of self-preservation. Domination through fear is an ongoing syndrome, one that has been perpetrated on humanity since the time of altered consciousness in Atlantis, when Annunaki intervention changed the course of humanity, and the yin-dominant society, nurturing and intuitive, was suppressed by the omnipotent male vibration of power and aggression.

You have been trained to fear even God, to believe 'he' will punish you if you sin, and to fear love, for you can be betrayed or abandoned. Throughout history, you have seen demonstrated the fear of knowledge, with the deliberate burning of the great libraries. The Wisdom contained in the writings of the Adepts and Masters who have walked the Earth has always been the key to your liberation. How difficult, then, is it to create within you fear of extraterrestrial beings; fear of catastrophes from outer space; fear of the coming years of Earth's transformation? *You turn away; you refuse to look; you bury yourselves in ignorance*, while the latest discoveries of space and its extraterrestrial inhabitants are held secret amongst the élite who wish to own the Wisdom. They truly believe that, if they can generate fear within you while holding back the light of knowledge, they will keep the power. Here lies the key to your liberation from the controls of those who would own you:

> The devil is the fear you hold within you
> The Luciferian aspect of your existence
> Your chains, the darkness of ignorance
> Are your prison.
> *
> Understanding death and passage
> Birth and rebirth
> Initiates the process of your emancipation
> Your awakening…

Keeping you in isolation, rendering foolish and fantasmagorical the idea of your fraternity with galactic beings, has been the administrative plan of those who have controlled Earth from time immemorial. This is why you are denied truth, for once you, as a mass, accept the existence of life beyond the biological confines of your terrestrial parameters, you will outgrow your fences. Your minds will flourish with all the unimaginable possibilities of worlds beyond yours, and you will finally experience the true meaning of freedom. You will demand it.

Let us describe our viewing of human activity in space as we are now watching it unfold, but of which you are privileged to know a truly infinitesimal part. To begin with, we have news for you, in case you have not yet understood: **you are the extra-terrestrials of the future**.

Bear in mind, when you engage in animated debate over your beliefs regarding visitors from other planets, that your very astronauts, were they to be witnessed by other beings in space, would be seen arriving in unidentified flying objects, wearing strange-looking metallic suits and helmets, and carrying magical instruments and weapons. To a less-developed civilisation, they would undoubtedly appear to be of a superior intelligence, either to be revered or feared, determined by their actions. Your astronauts, in missions upon other celestial bodies, would engage in the activity of probing and studying the new environment, and this theorem finds confirmation in the fact that NASA's first activities on Mars and the lunar surface involved the gathering of mineral samples for laboratory analysis.

Imagine, now, the impact a simple cigarette lighter would have upon a being whose civilisation had never seen fire. Would it not be interpreted as a gift of the gods? And as has often been the nature of trade between peoples, your explorers would most likely be willing to teach the native beings their technology in exchange for access to their biological data. The discovery of life beyond Earth is supposedly the great quest of your space programmes — despite the fact that constant visitation and contact from other worlds has always occurred on the blue-green planet.

The Sumerian Texts, to cite one of many sources, refer repeatedly to the arrival of gods from the heavens dressed in strange clothing, wearing helmets and carrying weapons. You have much material to read from and many codes have been left for you.

Why haven't you been told of the more recent encounters with contemporary navigators of space? Their secrecy is based on a two-fold principle: first, that you are deemed incapable of coping, as we have previously suggested and second, they are hiding the fact that a dynamic exchange was reached between the greys and the Secret Government, who traded you as guinea pigs for alien technology — pure and simple. Know that your government's inter-action with alien intelligence flourished over fifty years ago, at the time of the incident known to you as *Roswell*, when an extra-terrestrial craft carrying three beings crashed in a field in New Mexico. One of these was saved, and went on to serve as tech-nical advisor to the military. The story has been 'leaked' to the public to prepare you for a time not too far in the future when the government will come clean on its long-term collaboration with these beings. They have been studying you, preparing for the mass reaction.

This direct interaction, the dark energies of an involuntary exchange which involved denying the free will of sentient beings in the universe, activated a portal from the grey zone. Soon many of those beings were pulled out of the void and freed to move about in your physical dimension — to serve as technicians in the experiments being performed upon Earth beings. The Secret Government was given some of the fundamental knowledge of unlimited space travel, which we have described to you as 'spin-ning disk technology' and with this, learned to manipulate the force of gravity. It was a fine trade for the Power, who received a wealth of information and all that was required of them was the betrayal of the human race — not a particularly difficult choice considering their past record.

This concept, this understanding of yourselves as the extra-terrestrials of the future, is important to your comprehension of what occurs when space voyagers come to Earth. Once you move beyond your obsession with the individual accounts of abduction and the experimentation performed by the greys; once you step outside of your fear to then look at it objectively, you may recognise that their conduct in space follows the exact patterns of those supposedly being enacted by visitors to your planet. Indeed, human behaviour towards animals is often much more brutal than the inquisitive probing of the grey technicians.

Returning now to the activities of NASA under the directives of the Secret Government, we ask you to consider what is actually happening on the Moon. Do you follow the activities of your space programmes, paying attention to the time sequences of their journeys into the beyond? Is it not a bit curious to you that billions upon billions of your tax dollars have been funnelled into the military's exploratory manned space missions, and yet most of their findings and official photographs are considered 'classified' information to which you (the financiers) are not allowed access? Considering the poverty and existential crises facing your westernised cultures, worse in those poor and underdeveloped nations, we cannot but ask you why such an outpouring of resources does not stir you to question your national policies. That kind of investment, redirected towards ecological pursuits, would be enough to reset the scales of Gaia's imbalance.

Flight after flight into mysterious space ... for what purpose? Surely, that first triumphant march upon the lunar surface and the penetrating rape of Luna's soil with the great banner — acts of irreverent conquest — should have led to exhaustive exploration. Yet, only a few landings were conducted in those early years of the Apollo missions because, you were told, there was nothing there but worthless rocks and dust.

Surely, you don't really believe that — do you?

Here is another scenario, a sixth-dimensional treatise on the observation of your military penetration of the Moon, which you may first dismiss as a science fiction fairy tale, but will soon discover is an accurate picture of what is actually going on out there in the lunar orbit. To begin with, contrary to what you've been told, your Moon is rich in minerals and resources that are of

primary importance to industry and the military, and so the insinu-
ation that nothing is there for humanity is sheer camouflage. They
have had to overcome the logistics of getting to those resources,
a challenge faced in the last century on Earth and overcome with
the plight brought upon Gaia from the Industrial Age, resulting in
the ruthless destruction of much of the natural heritage of your
planet. Now, just as they have stripped the Earth, they intend to
mine the Moon of its riches and there, too, they are developing
the methodology to remove the obstacles and 'dig in', to extract
what they want from Luna's inner being.

Water, the essential element for life in all of its manifestations,
has been located at a substantial distance below the lunar surface.
You are slowly being opened to the remote possibilities of water
existing there because they are preparing you for the eventuality
of a Moon-station where, supposedly, astronauts will be based for
extended periods of time to study and explore the lunar habitat in
the name of science and progress. This is being slowly cultivated
in your minds, in small doses, while full immersion penetration of
the sanctity of the Moon is already well past its initial phases.
Remember: *you are spoon-fed only as much as the Power believes
you can absorb.*

What you are not being told, what is by no means to be ren-
dered public domain, is that many of your space missions involve
secret journeys to the Moon. You haven't been told the truth about
your penetration of space, nor do you care ... for once a launch
has been accomplished, you rapidly lose interest in your flying
capsules. In becoming a routine extension of your aerospace
enterprise, space flight no longer fascinates you, and so you
simply haven't been looking. Ask yourselves when was the last
time you followed with any particular interest the journey of the
manned craft, the shuttle, or investigated NASA's probes of outer
space. There is much misinformation and silence, a blasé form
of journalism and television media coverage that does little to
stimulate your enthusiasm and interest.

In the meantime, they have been quite busy, your new explorers, creating the first manned lunar bases, which already house

the engineers, scientists and military experts who are now developing the Lunar Biosphere[1] — developed from the research and experimentation of a similar artificially created ecosystem which currently exists in the Gaian desert of Arizona. The land of the selected lunar site was surveyed for optimum surface conditions, there where natural structures in the Moon's surface and remaining bits of the ancient dome of the Annunaki colonies could be utilised to serve as protection against bombardment from space and as shields against observation. Strategic positioning of the Biosphere was also determined by the resources available, for there had to be ideal conditions for drilling of minerals and water directly from within the grounds, and that has been accomplished.

Satellites equipped with solar reflector panels have been placed in strategic positions above the site, which will beam reflected sunlight into solar energy panels being built into the dome, to provide simulated daylight for the flora and fauna of the community as well as additional energy. Underground hydroelectric generators will eventually be adapted to serve as the major power source.

Similar to techniques implemented in the war against Iraq, you have state-of-the-art technology being utilised in covert military manoeuvres and that which is occurring now on the Moon is no different, no more fantastic than what was conducted in that techno-war. It is just a new territory, the modern day virgin fields of still remote heavenly bodies, but it is the same management team holding the game plan.

Military scientists have also been working with technologies as yet unpronounced to you, to create favourable conditions there that will render the lunar climate and environment hospitable for human life and the proliferation of various animal species. Underground water supplies have, indeed, been located and preparations are underway now to pump the water through treatment plants at the surface: this will be accomplished in a very short time. Below the refracted rays of sunlight being beamed through the silicate shell of the artificial dome, the first generations of plant life (currently seeded in the hothouse scientific laboratory of the military base) have successfully sprouted and will be transplanted in the soil of the Biosphere — providing oxygen to support the community. Spinning disk technology, for example, can create gravity just as it can create anti-gravity, and again technology has resolved a fundamental problem of the colonisation of life on the Moon, for spinning disks are to be installed in the Lunar Biosphere, creating sufficient gravitational fields to simulate Earth-like G-force for all beings living under the sealed dome.

It is Genesis revisited, only the creator of this 'beginning' is the loveless human hand of power.

Recently, a zoological space expedition was conducted, and many species were dragged into the crowded NASA shuttle to be probed and studied (does this sound familiar?) for their response to weightlessness and other altered biological conditions for importing animals to the Moon is going to play a vital part in the colonisation process. Imagine, once water is pumped up to the surface, the spinning disks have been activated to create gravitational fields within the community and solar and hydroelectric energy stations have been designed and made operative, the Biosphere will be able to host many life forms of which animals are a most integral part. We are afraid that the destiny of many of those species who are transported to the Biosphere will be less blessed than the beasts of the Ark. Those which escape the torture of the probes and poisons of the scientists, the gravity wheels and cages, will suffer in the artificial conditions of the eco-laboratories of the Biosphere. Their intuitive animal senses will cause them to behave in strange and erratic ways that will subject them to further torture and experimentation, for no artificial habitat can replace the sweet call of the wind in the trees, or the murmur of a brook as it snakes its way through the cool shadows below the forest's canopy.

Remember, too, that the future residents of the most expensive real estate in the universe do love their New York Steaks and eggs, their milk and honey cakes and tea. They do not intend to do without the 'creature' comforts. Unlike the blessed beasts who journeyed to foreign lands aboard Noah's Ark, the tortured animals traversing space will be probed and tested, or harnessed to serve. Their genetic material, however, will be preserved to clone various species in a later phase of colonisation, once the survival habitats have been established.

Now, if you can conceptualise from its inception the idea that your Secret Government has mastered its understanding of spinning disk technology and is already utilising it in its secret space missions (the parallel space programme of which you still have been told nothing), you might consider that what you are told of the NASA launches is only a front for the real activities of their programmes — and that is the case. Having learned with alien technology the conquest of gravity, they are now capable of carrying heavy materials and equipment to the Moon, for that was another obstacle to be overcome when plans to colonise were first developed.

In these preliminary years, supplies and tools are essential to the construction of life support structures there. Your standard spacecraft would never have been able to sustain the additional weight on board, for the constraints of gravity and fuel storage demand a highly streamlined vehicle. But now, you understand from our discussion of spinning disk technology in flying saucers that all that is contained within the craft becomes weightless as well, therefore eliminating the problem of transport in space. Know that they possess a fleet of saucer-like craft, designed and built in that military installation known as Area 51, and that these human extraterrestrials are moving about regularly in space (in the very flying saucers that you, in your innocence, believe to be commanded by visitors from other worlds), while simultaneously, they are officially pursuing the now obsolete methodology of standard space travel. Metaphorically speaking, they are creating the setting whereby you can daydream of a future of humankind's extension into space, while they are already sleeping in their feathered beds upon the Moon.

You can imagine how delighted those of the Power are to have found such a perfect cover for their free penetration of your night skies, and if you are encouraged to pursue the UFO phenomenon it is because it serves the establishment — it is the ultimate smoke-screen. We trust you find great irony in the idea that while you are marvelling at what appear to you to be spaceships from the beyond, there are, in many instances, actually human beings manning the controls. It would seem that the joke, as you say, is on you.

Once water had been found below the Moon's surface, and the problem of transporting essential building materials, tools and food supplies had been overcome, the evacuation solution of those of the Secret Government and their chosen representatives was initiated, and work begun. Plans for their migration off Pianeta Terra have been set at 2010, when the Biosphere will be fully integrated and a comfortable sojourn can be guaranteed to those of the 'Members Only' residences there, upon the far side, where probes and tracking units cannot penetrate.

It is their intention to wait out the Earth Changes that are prophesied for 2012, until the destructive forces of Earth's up-heaval have calmed, and all is once again a fertile field to be rebuilt through their might and technology. In their delusions of power and physical immortality, they do actually foresee a gallant return to an Earth that will now be their total dominion ... to rebuild and repossess all that remains of the New Lands of Armageddon. Do you see the plot unfolding: the return of the gods? From their hermitage in space, the élite will be organising their return to Earth, elaborating the new structures of their power, while you, the masses of inconsequential humanity, drown and disappear from the surface of Gaia.

These individuals, having conducted humanity to trash the Earth for profit and power, still do not understand that all is con-nected, all is karmically bound. With closed hearts, they observe the results of their abuse, recognising that their experiment has failed and mutated, and still their most urgent Earth management issue is the assurance of their own survival and that of their seed, the future power élite. For they have learned nothing. They refuse to understand that there is no escaping karma, for so fixated are they in their worship of power that they believe themselves above universal order. They have separated themselves from Prime Creator — from the animals, Gaia and all living things — and yet know not that it is from themselves, from their own hands, that they must be delivered.

These individuals' desperate leap into the fabricated haven of the Lunar Biosphere, they have yet to understand, will be their final frontier, for in the process of Solar Deity's journey through the astral chords, they are going to be left behind, spinning off into the darkest corners of the grey zone, for that is their karmic destiny. And so, those who have held the strings of humanity — manipulators from the earliest civilisations of the people of Gaia — are destined to be flung out into the great void, cast off their mother ship, the Moon, and into the silent cloud. There, as renegades of the universe, will they be inexorably linked to their alter-egos, the greys, throughout what you know to be eternity. The end of the cycle.

The joke, it seems, will be not be yours alone to bear.

Note

1. Richard Hoagland offers extensive documentation regarding the pre-existent archaeological remains of a dome-like, glassy structure that he directly parallels to this second Biosphere. See 'Recommended Reading'.

Twelve

OF LUCIFER AND DARKNESS

Annunaki
The Greys
The Secret Government
The Space Conspiracy
Genetic Manipulation

We have deliberately exposed and openly discussed some of the darker elements of what we deem your true reality to first provide you with relevant information, and then provoke you into looking at that which evokes feelings of fear within you. How else will you move through that fear unless you are first willing to shed some light upon it? To pull it all up into consciousness, you must look at and experience the elements of the darkness and then bathe them in light ... for the looking is, of its own, an act of healing the emotions and releasing them. It is taking charge, understanding and making clear the unclear; it is empowering yourselves as prime movers of your individual realities.

You, the magicians, create your world as you move through it. Some are content to pull the rabbit from the hat; others are intent upon performing the Great Work, whereby you bring yourselves up to the gold of your awakened light bodies. We are delighted to observe and experience many pockets of light ones strung across the planet now, a glittering cincture of golden beads and diamond lights, which encircles the Goddess and radiates her luminescence throughout the bodies of Solar Deity and out into the Cosmos. Your numbers are growing, and as you multiply and unite, the light of Gaia shines more lustrous through the heavens.

It is a breathtaking sight to behold.

The more you shine the brilliance of knowledge and love through the penumbra of your fear-dominated consciousness, the freer you become from your states of self-condemnation. In so doing, you diminish the effects of negative thought programmes that have been fed into the subconscious pools of your impressionable minds, for that is the way fear takes hold within you. And negative thought programmes there are, indeed, for you have been indoctrinated not only since birth (as we intend your physical emergence into the present lifetime), but since the very roots of your ancestral consciousness — your inception as the race of Earth men and women, children of the stars.

From the first Annunaki intervention in the Great Experiment (the stripping of your DNA) to the raping of your Goddesses — you have experienced violent administration of your mental, emotional and physical bodies from sources who intended to own you, as if possession of the beings of Gaia came with the property. You have been taught fear, obedience and separation so that you could be controlled and harnessed to serve the Annunaki and their lineage: to mine the resources of Gaia, build the machinery and amplify the lower vibrations of your animal bodies out into their fields. This, to feed their power, their greed and lust, for those lower chakra energies still dominate your planet and have continued to fuel them since the Annunaki's early intervention amongst you.

Why do you think the quest for inner beauty and love has been suppressed in your societies? We speak of self-love and the unconditional love which emanates from your heart centres, rather than the sexual, emotional bonding predominant in your current relationships — but which, from its conditioned responses creates much disharmony in your lives. Unconditional love, where everything about the other is beautiful simply because that one exists, is the **heart**. You, the awakening, are learning much about loving from that centre, for you are opening now to the One Heart of the universe, moving up into the higher vibrations. Instead, that manifestation of what the unenlightened like to term 'love', which emanates from the chakric wheel of desire and sensuality, inevitably reflects the instability of the emotional body. It is the swinging back and forth of feelings as they are dependent upon reciprocal expressions from the other.

As most of the human population is emotion-centred in its expression of love, we see much suffering and misunderstanding in the human union. There, where there could be shared the joy of total acceptance and respect between you, are more often manifested competition, positioning and the bartering of emotions, sexuality and power.

Think now ... think carefully. Any time in your history that art, music and poetry have prevailed — moments of hope and inspiration, the 'higher' aspects of humanity — ugliness has manifested as a force that moves in to suppress their expression and push you back into despair and resignation. Why is that so? Consider the wealth of wisdom and illumination lost forever in the burned athenaeum of Alexandria and other great libraries of civilisations known and yet unknown to you, for destroying your intellectual and artistic manifestations helps stimulate the beast within you. You build and then tear down your monuments; you write and then burn your ideals; you love your neighbours and then kill the enemy.

When you are loving and full of celebration of life and its beauty, or inquisitive and philosophical about the human condition, you are not fulfilling your duties: serving the master. You are not on your knees: obeying. Don't you find it most ironic that your exoteric religions have you kneeling at the shrines and altars? We have come to challenge you to question whether or not it is high time you rose to your feet, reaching your arms up to the heavens in celebration of the God-force that you can see and feel all around you, within and beyond: in the trees, and riding upon the wind; in the faces of others; the eyes of the doe; a child's laughter; the Sun.

We are calling you to arise from your knees and stand tall against the winds of change, for your fears can only be conquered when, as free-thinking men and women, you understand that you are the Power and the blessing and the light. Your very architecture teaches you that the soles of your feet are meant to contact the earth, and we remind you that that is how you draw the power and the music of Gaia, the *wam*, into your souls.

Soles for the soul. Your language provides you with many morphological clues to the mysteries.

Most physicians agree that the knees are the weak link of your bodies, for they are weighed down and weakened by gravity, body mass and the simple wear and tear to which you subject them throughout your lifespans. We wish to suggest, if even from a purely logistical point of reference, that you give them a rest. From the metaphysical aspect, we view the knees as your point of obedience, resignation, fear and servitude, and we assure you that a loving God would not encourage these energies within you. Why then, we ask, are you kneeling in the temples?

Arise, star gazers! When you plant your feet firmly upon the soil you are capable of pulling the strength of the Goddess through your bodies and into your souls. Standing tall now, call the light through your crowns, and there where the forces of the Earth and the stars unite within you, feel the golden explosion within your hearts. Experience yourselves at centre, the stilled pendulum, and now listen. Can you hear the bass chord of Gaia?

Is it any wonder that you are fearful as a race? You hold fear, the polar opposition of trust, within you from so very long ago that it is as if that emotion has become permanently embedded within your coding. You have been genetically manipulated, trapped in the net, and taught to believe that you are the orphans of the universe. That has been done to you deliberately, for as gods in your own right you would have been uncontrollable, free-thinking beings … and that was not acceptable to them then, at the seeding, nor now, as the descendants of the Annunaki struggle with the greatest power play of their existence.

Consider those great leaders of your recent days, whose all-too-brief appearance in the Earth realm manifested in roles of leadership that were intent upon helping you break free: Gandhi, Anwar Sadat, John F. Kennedy, his brother Robert, Martin Luther King, Yitzhak Rabin, Mikhail Gorbachev and others. Even the Christed One, Jesus of Nazareth, was a revolutionary who rebelled against the Authority and the religious hierarchy of his time to show you the way to the Kingdom within. Have you forgotten? These light ones encouraged peace on your planet, brotherhood and unity amongst you. They were simply too dangerous a voice, for their clarity, conviction and charisma were enough to affect behaviours of disobedience and inspire your desire for true liberation — and the Power knew it. For this, they were eliminated.

You are neither stimulated nor educated to the true pursuit of equality, freedom and your right to question the Authority. You are only allowed the illusion of your independence, and that concession is made only because the Power knows you must have some ray of hope in order to operate efficiently for them. Otherwise, you shut down completely, becoming totally ineffectual and eventually rebelling, as witnessed within those dictatorial demographical boundaries (which you refer to as 'countries'), where the people have been held in total submission. They have learned from experience that it is much easier to control you by feeding your fantasies of liberty; the subtle manipulations of the media and communications are much more effective management tools than the omnipotence of the ball and chain.

In the perpetual unfolding of karma, however, the wheel is turning and now it is they, the power élite, who fear — for they do realise to some extent what is happening. They know that they are on the brink, about to slip into the void of the grey zone, because they realise the experiment is almost over and Earth is dying. You, the human race, are tiring of the materialistic paradigm that for so long has motivated you to achieve their ends and, therefore, they are scrambling for a solution, for soon there will be nothing left to take from you.

Because karma has bound them to your planet they are desperate, and it is from that desperation that is born the 'last resort option'. This is the evacuation plan to retreat to the Lunar Biosphere and wait out Earth's tumultuous revolution, to then return and pick up where they left off. After all, their ancestors inhabited the Moon ... and so can they. They have the tools, the materials and technology to create the survival habitat, and the memory. They have the pre-existing structures, as demonstrated to you through the probing works of the Adept, Richard Hoagland, whose videos have shown you remnants of the dome from which they will reconstruct the city. We wish to remind you once again that evidence of these structures exists as actual photographic images taken from your most 'reliable' source: NASA, your government's space agency.

You can understand why they would prefer to keep this their little 'Top Secret', can't you?

This is the Emergency Plan as it plays out in their survival strategy: a Patrician community of Earth's top administrators, the 'crème de la crème', all comfortably safe in their lunar beds while Gaia, victim of their directed abuse, breaks down and the plebeians are cleared out of the way. With time, all then slowly comes back to centre and the renegades, the new gods, return again to rebuild their empire and guide what is left of humanity back into the nets and back onto your knees.

They do not understand what is taking place now in your Solar Deity's body, because they are so bound to the third dimension that they cannot conceive of the ascension of the entire solar system, but they are fearful, for their planet was long ago cast out of its orbit by just such a celestial event. They cannot imagine that many of you will move up along with the planet, while they remain imprisoned in their own karma. Moreover, they are so convinced of your inferiority that they cannot accept your progression into higher states of being, while they remain in the darkness clinging to the physical. Or worse, being flung into the void, the grey zone, trapped between dimensions.

They have yet to understand the nature of Spirit ... that all is in a state of becoming, of moving up. Even they are evolving towards the light, however slowly. This is a key to your under-standing of duality and polarity, and this knowledge will be most crucial to your ascension once you truly incorporate it into your awareness:

> **Even the darkest beings**
> **reflections of All-That-Is**
> **Journey the spiral of ascension**
> **eventually moving into the Light**
> **for that is the nature of Spirit.**

You are emerging from the shadows of your past, becoming free beings in every sense of the word, but first you must pass through the blackness, the process of exploring your deepest fears as a people and as individuals. You must have courage and conviction; then, as you exhibit your strength in confronting those dark corners within you, will you realise that your fears are unfounded and empty. It will be necessary that you speak your truth freely; that you question the dogma of accepted thought, religion and government; and that you release yourselves from the enchainment of consumerism and the feeding of the animal within you.

Just as important will be your acceptance of these attitudes in others: your responsiveness to the ideas and philosophies that develop around you, which you are free to accept or discard at will. What matters is that your minds remain open to the truth of others as well as your own, for once you become set in your con-victions, you lose the fluidity of thought and the receptivity to change which mark the accelerated heart/mind of the Aquarian.

Moreover, you need to learn forgiveness, for that is the great-est expression of your Godhood. Know that every being — every single being — is on that spiral with you. In all dimensions, regardless of how intensely some may cling to their dark cloaks, there is always a spark of light within them. We have told you that light is consciousness and all beings are, on some level, consciously aware. We are united in our journey, moving home. Some choose to give enormous energy to the darkness, others move quickly into the light, but that again is a reflection of free will. Trust that it is so, and that you are free to forgive and accept those who remain behind. Rather than fear the darkness, you can shine the light into it. These are the choices you are making now that you are accelerating onto higher vibrational levels and experiencing such great expansion in the heart.

Seek out the beauty that is abundant all around you, rather than pore into the ugliness of your sensational media tales and those holographic images of violence and depravity conveyed through your televisions and computers. Seek beauty and you will find it. What are you waiting for? You are entitled to the knowledge that has been held from you; it is yours to receive and share, and now more than ever the networks are opening to you. You have the right and the capacity to shine the light into the dark corners of your ignorance and release yourselves and the planet from that hold. Otherwise, all the work that you undertake as spirit journeyers will be futile and ineffective. Until you enter into the caves of your darkest terror and let flow forever the stagnant waters of your memory, you will not make it into the white light, where polarity resolves and so the darkness. Unless you help guide others to the same discoveries you will achieve little from your solitary realisations, for love is to be shared. The Light knows no limitation.

The supreme fear, the greatest of your terrors as physical beings, appears to be the fear of death, which we have addressed in other moments of these transmissions. You know now that only by coming to terms with death and your own immortality can you release the greatest of your apprehensions. Your embracing of the Eastern religions and growing acceptance of the karmic process are helping you to comprehend your eternal return and transformation. Indeed, understanding reincarnation greatly facilitates the calming of that primordial beast, the fear of non-existence.

But what of the devil, the quintessential evil force? You begin with the premise, an understanding, that everything that exists is a reflection of *The All-That-Is, That-Has-Ever-Been and That-Always-Will-Be*, and very early on in your religious and philosophical training you are indoctrinated into the dogma in such a way that you are blinded to the paragon of the evil archetype as the antithesis of Supreme Being.

Have you never asked yourselves: if all is God, the All-That-Is, then how do we account for a devil, great counterpart of the God-force? How can anything emerge as separate, when all is One? And yet, how can one reconcile evil within God? God, all that which is good and blessed, containing the devil within it? To say that religion contradicts itself is sublime understatement. Herein lies the philosophical paradox of your religions, for you see that the devil, an evil force to be conquered and dominated, simply doesn't fit in the paradigm of God as *The All-That-Is, That-Has-Ever-Been and That-Always-Will-Be*; and you find you have a philosophical dilemma on your hands, to say the very least.

We have come to a point in these teachings where we feel we must expose the Luciferian paradox as a glitch in your belief structures. Therefore, we wish to restate the obvious: if you believe in God, Supreme Being, the All-That-Is, how can you account for a separate force: a devil? In the All-That-Is, how can anything else 'be'? There is a contradiction of terms in your most common religions that God is above, beyond and within all things — while the devil, evil of all evils, works alone.

Your Bible doesn't tell it that way, does it? In the less adulterated versions of your religious books you have clearer insight into the workings of Lucifer, the fallen angel, who agrees to serve the darkness to assist humanity — to provide you with the free will parameters that constitute existence as an individual soul consciousness. That message is blurred to your vision, for it has been made unclear through the various interpretations placed upon those holy scriptures. You would do well to reread the Bible as a story of empowerment and knowledge, rather than the tool that it has been made into by religious culture: a mythical manual of obedience. We are telling you that this great work of esoteric mysticism holds all the Secret Wisdom, but that your religious leaders distort the teachings into new paradigms that serve their structures. You must read past their teachings, returning to the core information that lies within the writings and break the codes, revealing the intended meaning of the words, before they were transmuted into their current interpretations.

Wasn't it the Bible that introduced the evil snake in the magical garden? His words to Eve urged her and Adam to partake of the forbidden fruit, which would 'open their eyes forever, to become as gods — knowing good and evil'. You have been taught to fear the snake and to believe that your troubles started when Adam and Eve disobeyed God and here we are again, back at the power struggle, reliving the guilt that is not yours to bear. That interpretation has you fearing the condemnation of God ... 'His' wrath upon those who dare to disobey divine law and rule. On the other hand, we ask you: what would have become of the only two beings in existence had they resisted the apple and remained the sole residents of the pleasure garden?

There is a different message to be read from those words, those sacred teachings, and we ask you to hear a quite different interpretation. — a sixth-dimensional treatise on these archetypes — where the snake (Satan, the shadow self of God) encourages Eve (the yin, intuitive self) and Adam (the yang, logical, analytical self) to recognise that they are sparks of the divine light, responsible for their free will choices and that from the apple (the fruit of that awareness), they are free to choose between the polar extremes of good and evil, light and dark, God and Satan.

The one interpretation teaches you fear and guilt; the other empowers you to know the God-force within you. Is it any wonder the Power has favoured the prior?

The religious leaders call you to your knees to obey God and fear the devil, or whatever evil counterpart reflects a given religion's expression of the opposition to the God-force. It is always a form of Satan, the antagonistic element in all religions, and throughout time, in even the most pagan cultures, evil spirits have been chased away, cast out, feared and revered. Without evil, there is no religion, is there? That is, if religion is to exist, doesn't it need an antagonist to create the dynamic tension so necessary to the human tragedy?

Consider Greek theatre or your own modern films and dramatic plays. Without the dynamic contrast, protagonist/antagonist, good/bad and ugly ... there is no plot that can hold one's attention. Billions upon billions of dollars are required to maintain the great and profitable institutions of organised religion in your world, and they too, must hold your interest to insure the flow of capital into the coffers. There where your places of worship are covered in gold domes and untold riches, your total conviction that the conflict between good and evil exists becomes a necessary prelude to your donations and tithing. Our question to you: would you be so willing to fall upon your knees and obey the priests and ministers if there were no potential evil from which to be saved?

Imagine, for a moment, what would be required to fulfil the role of opposition to the light of the God-force. What kind of spirit being would be willing to take on such an assignment? Bear in mind, now, that if you believe in the All-That-Is, then you must by definition believe that Lucifer is part of that totality, and you can only be left to deduce the obvious ... that the evil Lucifer, dark pole of the God-light, is actually a **reflection** of that light. The devil, an aspect of the All-That-Is, then serves you, for the very nature of this dark side offers you, conscious men and women, the free will choice. This is what separates you from the animals; this is the fundamental reason of your existence.

The darkness, then, must be redefined and you can do that once you remove your fear of death and evil. Again, we remind you that only ignorance can hold you in chains, and that when you explore your shadows and accept that even the darkness serves humanity, you will truly be operating in the light.

Most religions of your civilisation have driven the fear so deep within you that it is going to be a monumental task, overthrowing the devil and then embracing an understanding of his dynamic relationship to God. In our first communication, we spoke to you of the sacred darkness. When you understand, you can forgive those who choose to hold the dark vibration … forgiving the devil himself, and then incorporate them into your plans of unity and integration, for the two poles are **the whole**.

'Love your enemy,' said the Christed One. Did you understand the profound meaning of his message?

Are not the very Annunaki and their progeny the depiction of evil? We have not spared you warnings and caution regarding their intent. They, too, by definition, fall into the totality of the All-That-Is, and again you are shown by their very existence that you are the prime movers of your own realities. You can choose. That pole of darkness exists to give you this choice, to offer you the challenges of existence as gods in your own right, before you return to the absolute Oneness. For countless millennia of their control, you have chosen to obey, however forced and manipulated to it. Now, in the light of this great transformation, you are freer than ever to choose not to, but it remains a choice that you, conscious beings, must make. Many prefer the darkness, content to remain imprisoned in their ignorance, fear and rage. Others choose the light, knowing that knowledge and love break the chains.

That freedom to choose between good and evil is what makes sense of experience, for if there were no polarity whatsoever, could there exist free will? If you were only to know the light, what purpose would life serve? Where would you find your motivation? Indeed, were there no battles to fight, no difficulties to surmount, no choices to make … would there be any reason to exist, to separate from the God-self? You, as sparks of divine light, break away from the Godhead to develop as individual entities; to know your own godliness; to exist. And then, having faced the challenges of that will, return to the entirety — the brilliance.

In the polarity of your existence, you are learning that the ends of the spectrum are simply complimentary aspects of the whole: love/hate; hot/cold; good/evil. These are dynamic expressions of the One, and although you believe you can experience one side of the pole without the other, that is a wrong concept. Poles offer you the exaltation of their reflections; that is, when you experience misery then do you understand joy; when you have drowned in tears then do you know the absolution of laughter. Pain is to pleasure what wrong is to right, what no is to yes ... each aspect is dependent upon the other for its identity.

It is your human experience, living these polar compliments in your emotions and in some ways we are envious, for we do not experience the emotional body as do you. The intensity of your feelings eludes us. Even in your pain, you do enjoy experiencing the emotionality of your suffering, for it is the intensity of human emotion that drives you to move mountains and reach forever beyond your limitations. Unfortunately, the emotional body of humankind weighs with a predominance of the lower vibrations at this time when so much pain, fear and suffering dominate the planet. And yet, it doesn't have to be that way, as you, the awakening, have discovered.

You are changing the music and many are beginning to hear it for the first time.

And now, since we are asking you to explore the God-devil polarity (the good-evil duality), we cannot but draw your attention to the fact that as you enter Aquarian consciousness, you are witnessing extremes of light and dark in what you term the New Age movement. We have told you. There are those who have chosen the dark side, for these are the ones whose ego identities have not been released, and so they do not understand that they are not separate from you. The actions of the dark warriors eventually turn in upon themselves. In the meantime, they do serve you, for they provide the polarity from which choice is created.

You, the awakening, will be called upon to assist these beings, for all must move up. All will eventually be illuminated; this is simply the way of Spirit. Although so many have chosen to wallow in the blackness, you must always remember that every being is a reflection of the God-light. No matter how dim, it is there, for each bears the spark of creation. All beings hold within them the rainbow spectrum (the chakra system), however dull and lustreless their reflection. They can be reached.

If it is painful for you to imagine such an assignment, where you might be called to shine the light of your love and compassion into those darkest shadows, remember that you, too, at some time during your long journey, have drunk of the dark wine.

Thirteen

LIVING THE FOURTH DIMENSION

We would like you to think of the closing down of the polarity of your dimension as its refinement, for if you can imagine shades of experience rather than opposites, then perhaps you will understand the subtle metamorphosis of the physical, emotional and mental bodies as it occurs in a dimensional shift. In the fourth, you move up in awareness to a level where you are forever experiencing the oneness of all vibration, and that heightened sense of the totality and interdependency of all existence cannot help but alter your expression and understanding of the free will arena. As such, what appears as an either/or framework to you now, in the third dimension, becomes diffused into shades of the One in your evolved consciousness as fourth dimensional beings.

Many of the teachers and leaders of your Age are speaking now of the end of polarity and that is actually in error, for the duality of which we have spoken in detail **must** exist at some level, if you are to know the freedom of independent action ... of choice. It is the motivational driver of your existence — your evolutionary trigger. Again, we refer to the beautiful ones, Adam and Eve of the mythical garden, to develop a fundamental philosophical point. Had they not committed the great 'sin' of choosing to eat the apple, they would have become bored and listless in paradise — condemned to an eternity of passivity and inertia. As divinity incarnate, they would have had no cardinal reason to exist — no purpose for which to separate from the All-That-Is and make their way beyond the garden of eternal light and perfection.

Even more compelling, speaking always in metaphor of Adam and Eve and disobedience, is the realisation that without 'sin', there would have been no human race — for if they had not eaten of the forbidden fruit they most certainly would not have indulged in sexual union. In the end, what purpose would their existence have served? Could it be that Supreme Being would have created such a vacuous duo just to have them aimlessly wander through eternity as his obedient servants, prototypes of a race that was never to be? Would you truly consider that a blessing, or an act of love ... or intelligence? Surely it would make no sense in the cosmic scheme of things and as such plays out as a dead-end in what we know is a constantly evolving universe.

No, only in that crisis moment, when Eve confronted the Shadow and accepted responsibility for her very existence, did life take on meaning and purpose. Eve, the archetype of the intuitive half of your 'universe', convinced Adam (your logical minds), to trust that God willed upon them their individuality ... their existence as extensions of the Godhead, conscious beings who would be responsible for their independent, free-will decisions.

Sirian analysis of the creation myth sees the intuition correctly guiding and influencing the logic, an interpretation which overturns your religious establishment's rendition of the Adam and Eve story. That scenario depicts poor Adam resisting as best he could Eve's weakness in the face of temptation and then eventually giving in to her 'sinful desire', and in so doing, defying God. In this version, logic attempts to overrule the erring intuition and losing, suffers the condemnation caused by the unforgivable error — defiance of God's mandate to 'look but not touch' the tree of golden fruits.

Through this distorted interpretation of the Eden myth, the exoteric ministers are warning you that you must not trust your intuition, that you are not gods in your own right and that you are incapable of knowing truth. It is the obedience fundamental, over and over again, for here is another aspect of the dogma that positions God outside of you, while enforcing the belief that only through obedience can you be assured absolution.

Who you were programmed and manipulated into obeying, by now, we believe we have made clear to you. However you wish to identify the hierarchy to whom you have given your power in the past, remember that it is the exalted yang, male energy of the clerics, whose historic interpretations of the Garden of Eden present you with a victimised Adam who, tantalised by the temptress, is lured into disobedience by the persuasive yin force. Their equation plays out so that Eve becomes the equivalent of sin; the archetype of intuition and inner knowing is condemned — the Goddess sabotaged!

Why? Let us suggest that your women have been systematically disempowered since the days of the Atlantean intervention, when the priestess power was so great: a time of nurturing of soul and enlightenment in what was the golden hour of humanity. The male population, having tired of centuries of female supremacy, were easily incited to rebellion — activated by the Annunaki warriors — and have held the pendulum since then, for well over 16,000 Earth years. This is why most myth and history, recorded by the men, have preserved the image of the woman as temptress, whore, mother and wife. Woman as Goddess-power appears only in those fragments of Earth's recorded history when humankind reached great intellectual and spiritual heights.

Yet, you know that it is the intuitive mind, that feeling, psychic side of you, that is connected: that is the part that reaches out of 3D and onto higher levels. The logical mind of external influences often confuses you, distracting you from the clarity of the inner voice. As we expose the archetypal dwellers of Eden then, do you see how Eve (the yin self) is teaching Adam (the logic) that the way of free will is the way to true existence?

Embedded within the dynamic depiction of Adam and Eve and the polarity of good and evil is the equilateral cross, the fundamental symbol of your mystical libraries and absolute foundation of the Secret Wisdom.

Within this simple model lies the blueprint of the structure of polarity, for through it you are shown the dualities of the microcosm (your conscious reality) as they interconnect with the polar opposites of the macrocosm (the All-That-Is). As you explore this principle, you recognise that when you are at centre of your being — that perfect balance of the yin/yang aspects of personality — you are, by definition, at centre of Spirit. You may wish to reread our message regarding the seven directions, for that passage will now take on a more profound meaning to you, as you realise that by going within, you will have reached the epicentre of all experience, escaping duality in all of its manifestations.

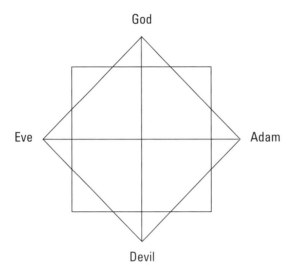

That the God/devil tension is but a reflection of your polar experience is mirrored to you through this diagrammatic representation of (wo)man and God. We believe that by studying and meditating upon its form, you will accelerate your resolution of polarity consciousness, enabling you to ride out the extremes of its manifestation in the Desert Days of Gaia's transition. You must understand how you create and reflect that duality in your world before we can explain how life without such extremes will unfold for you in the heightened fields of fourth-dimensional reality.

If you are having difficulty accepting this paradigm into your consciousness because you feel that it conflicts with what you have embraced as the 'holy cross' of the Christ, please be aware that we are speaking here of the **equilateral cross**, where all four segments are of the same length and that is a totally different symbol. This is extremely relevant as you develop a keener awareness of Sirian form, number and equation. From this most profound of your esoteric symbols emerges another key:

> Only by integrating the
> yin and the yang aspects of your own being
> will the illusion of polarity of Spirit resolve.
> When the Adam and Eve within you
> become One
> Then can you know and understand
> the All-That-Is.

Like Adam and Eve, you still need the duality, for there are many choices you must create for yourselves if you are to proceed on your evolutionary path. Only when you, co-creators of the universe, have evolved to a point where you are melding back into the Godhead, will you no longer require polarity to exist. As you reach completion of your soul journey (the God-self that has expressed the desire to exist as individual consciousness) you will be entirely freed of the quintessential requirement of self-conscious existence: the free-will motivator and your evolutionary driver — **choice**.

What is important is that, as you move through the higher dimensions, the extremes in that inherent dualism become softened, for your understanding becomes such that you see the Whole, the overall, in the dynamic. Good and bad become aspects of being, no longer in opposition to each other, but rather fluctuations or shades of mutual expression. With the lifting of the veil, the archetypes of opposition disappear and so does the devil, being of absolute evil, for the extreme darkness of the fallen angel will no longer be relevant to you. You simply will not need that illusion to keep you on the balancing path between right and wrong, for you will no longer be limited to the either/or possibilities of that duality. Further, you will have processed so much of your fear once you pass through and survive the tunnel, the instantaneous rebirthing of your Solar Deity, that you will most likely have released it all well before you reach the bright light.

Can you imagine life without right and wrong? If you accept that all is in a state of upward movement and that the God-force permeates all things, then how can anything be wrong to begin with? As you are freed from the trappings of duality, the black and white of your current beliefs and behaviours, you move into an enlightened state of consciousness where you perceive the reciprocity in all things. Many of you have already developed your awareness to the point that you understand this mutual relationship, as is best depicted in the T'ai-chi T'u, symbol of the yin/yang dynamic. There you see the circle (symbol of the entirety) separated, in a graphic sense, into dark and light — in the same expression a point of darkness exists within the light and vice versa. This most significant design describes without words the perfectly interpenetrating relationship of polar aspects that comprises the whole.

Duality, then, neither ends at the closing of the Gaian calendar nor disappears in the higher dimension. Rather, it becomes clear to your consciousness, indeed, to your total experience, that polar forces are but the extremes of the whole — interdependent upon each other for existence. Rather than eliminating the poles, you will be refining them, in what we suggest will be a gradual process. In doing so, you integrate the extremes of polar opposition, and the devil — great 3D antagonist — disappears into the light of the all-pervading God-force: the Lucifer conflict resolves.

As difficult as it is for many of you to conceptualise, you will know gratitude to this Keeper of the Dark Energy for having served you as such a dedicated teacher, as he held the anchor of the opposition pole. Without him, you would never have been stimulated into breaking away and experiencing your own will. Like Adam and Eve, you would have known nothing more than an eternity of sunny days, quiet nights and absolute inertia.

You believe Jesus died for your sins? We suggest that the dark angel suffered the depths of darkness to teach you the freedom of choice.

We acknowledge that many of you have long understood this dynamic; we do not wish to imply that we are revealing unknown secrets. Rather, it is our intention to elucidate the new paradigms of fourth-dimensional consciousness, where all who ascend will know the experience of mutual relationship in every moment of their being. Can you imagine the freedom and the love that come from knowing that everything exists within every other, just as the energies of others exist within you? Separation disappears forever, and with it, so does your alienation, your orphanage and your fear.

We hear your question ringing out to us, 'What will it be like to leave the Earth and ascend to the fourth dimension?' To begin with, we hope we have made clear to you the fact that Earth moves through as an ascending celestial body, so that you are still Earth-centred in the higher dimension. In essence, you won't leave Gaia ... you will mutate with her. You worry about form; we can tell you that much of your perception will be so subtly altered that you will barely recognise that you are no longer in the physical. Those of you who choose to ascend the spiral as Earth residents will still be confronted with Gaia as she recovers from the extremes of human abuse and disharmony, and you will be dedicating much of your thoughts and energies to healing her. You will still love, emote and experience life in many ways as you do at this point of your development, but there will be many shades of change in your awareness ... many, many changes, indeed.

You are working towards becoming masters of your realities, extracting yourselves from the exoteric structures that dominate and manipulate you and now, more than ever, you need to rely upon your own perceptions and accumulated experience to move through your new realities. The Eve, your intuitional awareness, will take centre stage and most of your impressions will come through that aspect. The Adam, your logical minds, will relax, yielding once again to Eve ... letting the intuition override the logic. Earth will evolve as well, as the disharmony that she brings through the black hole will begin by definition to heal, for without your egos, separation and extreme emotions, you will come quite rapidly to harmony with Gaia.

The exoteric rulers, those who have directed you into obedience and fear, will most likely remain entrapped in the third dimension, experiencing the death process which will occur over large portions of your planet and incarnating on other celestial bodies of the physical universe at other times. Of these, some will join the power élite (those direct descendants of the Annunaki) as they move into the void of the grey zone. And you, the awakening, will transmute from the physical realm into your new experience of life as the interpenetrating of mind and events, where you will blend into the vibration of all the elements of consciousness in simultaneous existence.

Will you have physical bodies? Fear not, you will not lose your identities in the next phase! Do you understand what we intend by 'light bodies'? Your temples, the bodies that house your soul essence, will have been raised to higher frequencies, and that will bring new points of reference to your self-awareness, your perception of others, and your ability to recognise the cosmic waves that are passing through you. You will perceive each other's energies as vibrational fields, knowing in an instant the emotional and mental states of the other. You will be telepathic, free to communicate without words which are, in fact, limitations in your current experience.

We believe that, by now, you have accepted that our instrument brings a council of extraplanetary beings through to you on these pages. If not, you would already have put away this book. But is it the printed word or our vibrational codes that you are actually reading? Trydjya, a conscious energy being, does not simply perform as a robot bringing our rhetoric through her fingertips and into her computer. A consciousness unit, she experiences our thoughts in a form of telepathic synergy; she sees images as we transmit those waves across the screen of her third-eye vision, and then, as a physical being of your realm, condenses into words that which is our intended meaning. She is gifted … so are you, for within all conscious beings lies the potential of expansion and higher awareness. It is simply a matter of developing your skills and trusting the voice of your higher selves — your guidance — that determines how soon you, too, will open to receive the frequencies and that is part and process of your development.

In the fourth dimension, those skills become your common tools and you will all be opening, like fields of wild flowers feverishly bursting in the bloom of Spring. There will still exist degrees of awareness, for your individual abilities are only as developed as your soul is evolved. Your gifts are the rewards that you have earned through your spiritual accomplishments and the resolution of karmic debt. This is true of all dimensions and realities in the Cosmos, as we understand them. Just as you must face and over-come adversity in your process, so must you know the gratification of achievement, for these are the guidelines that show you the pathway home.

We know that you are looking for a practical, detailed picture of your future experience in the higher dimensions and that, despite the wealth of knowledge being made available to you now, there is still much allusion and little factual information regarding just what you are moving towards. Be patient. Remember that if you were to know all things before experiencing them, there would be no purpose to their acquisition. If you were to know the des-tination in its entirety, would you be so anxious to embark upon the journey? Anticipation of discovery is your greatest motivation, for once you break away from divinity, you begin the education process and you never stop learning — not even upon your return to the *All-That-Is, That-Has-Ever-Been and That-Always-Will-Be.* You understand that in returning you bring your acquired knowledge back into the All, and that was your intention from the very beginning.

Those of you who are about to enter the fourth-dimensional states of consciousness have been accepted into the Institute of Higher Learning ... Initiates in the experiential school of aware-ness. Having made the grade, you have earned many rewards and we can tell you that if you have not already begun to see, you will soon experience clairvoyant vision, for you will be seeing with the psychic eye, just as you will be hearing without physical ears and feeling without touch.

If you are already blessed with these gifts, you will soon notice your abilities have intensified, for that is simply the natural process, where all moves up. Your heightened senses become that much more acute as you proceed, for as you have been operating for some time on higher levels, you simply go higher. You have much to look forward to: you already know much about vibrational fields, thought emanations and etheric energies. You will be passing in and out of the fourth dimension with ease, reconnecting with your teachers and guides on even higher planes.

We know that it is of great concern to you that you still experience and enjoy sexual interaction in this new dimension. Know that your lower chakras are just as significant to the spectrum of light as are the higher vibrations of your rainbows. As beings of the fourth dimension, you continue to pro-create, although the forms change. With the refinement of your energies (a process you have already begun as awakening beings on the Earth plane), the sexual exchange becomes more of a heart experience, for once you know orgasm as great waves of ecstatic light moving through the cosmic sea, you become aware of its true significance. You will feel the energy race through your hearts with such intensity and rapture that you will wonder how you could ever have enjoyed such union in your animal selves, where physical pleasure and the ego gratification of conquest limit your experience to four or five seconds of physical release and the fleeting pleasure of momentary emotions.

Children will be born from your unions in light body. Remember that birth is the passing of a soul from one state of being into another and beings of the fourth dimension enjoy and experience parentage, childhood and procreation. Life is constantly searching to break through, just as the God-force appears in every breath, every seed and upon every wave.

The first generation children of the ascension are to be the new Earth Keepers, and what remains to be done will be accomplished through their expanded love and communication centres. They will tone Gaia back to resonance, for they will be born to that task, just as you came to assist in the birthing. These highly developed souls are preparing now for entry, and many are coming in just before the vortex pulls you into its centre and through the tunnel.

As difficult as it is for you to believe ... technology as you know it will disappear, for you will no longer need it. Isn't that the way of evolution? Why limit yourselves to a great mechanical net when your communications networks lie within your cellular bodies, transmitting mind across the Gossamer Web and through the cosmic sea? Thoughts and their transmissions, data and all the wisdom of existence can be pulled into your awareness simply by catching thought waves — 'surfing' in its truest sense! You will soon know the irony of your imminent discoveries, recognising as antiquity the cutting-edge innovations of your contemporary mechanics and technology. That moment will be the 'real time' like you never imagined it!

We do hear your thoughts; your collective fear that the shift will bring you to some ghostly existence as mere light waves passing through an ambiguous, unreal sphere of 'being' somewhere out there in the Cosmos. That deep, unresolved fear is a subconscious memory of passing over the grey zone when you move and shift through the various birth and death experiences of your reincarnational cycles. Although your current conception of spatial relationships limits our descriptive expression of the grey zone, we can describe it as lying between dimensions or, more precisely, between states of being. It would be more accurate yet to explain it to you as a parallel universe, if you can work with that abstract term.

Every time you pass through the tunnel of death or birth, you are confronted with the void and must move quickly over it. You know the danger, for it is as close to non-existence as you can come in an otherwise vibrantly moving and expanding universe — a sort of polar reflection of the Garden of Eden. It exists in your cellular memory: memory that has been brought forward as race consciousness in the teachings of many religions, in Egyptian hieroglyphics and throughout the mythology of the many worlds which comprise Universal Being.

There, in the fourth dimension, you are going to be very much alive and actively participating in your unfolding karma and that of Gaia. You chose to take part in this great evolutionary drama and that makes you even more special. You will experience nature as the blossom of your godliness, and will devote much of your energies to replenishing the Garden. Clearly, you will be less centred in your physical bodies and therefore many aspects of your current experience are going to change. Your emotional bodies will be clearing, your polarity consciousness refined, and your needs as conscious beings diminished. In fact, the clutter disappears in the fourth; your obsession with possessions fades, for the ego becomes silenced at that level of awareness. Many of the trappings that currently fill your lives are but reflections of your ego identification, and you see that the need for them is going to disappear when you move out of the third dimension.

What you hold important takes on new heights and meanings as you move up the spiral. Beyond the sensate realm, you will no longer be waste-producing and inefficient consumers of energy. Food — your fuel — will be the light, and this is one of the most significant changes that we can openly describe to you. Imagine the body no longer requiring food as you know it to be; Hostess cupcakes, McDonald's hamburgers and even the most exquisite and refined cuisine of your world kitchens. Consider how much waste results from the body's requirement of foodstuffs, and know that the taking of food into the body disappears in the fourth dimension. That alone brings great relief to Gaia, for how much of your planetary pollution is a product of the food requirement and the waste it creates?

We speak not only of your bodies' disposal of waste, which you pump into your oceans and lakes and which has seeped deeper and deeper into the Earth's surface. You are drowning in it; Gaia is choking with it — gasping and sputtering. What of the lungs of Gaia ... the trees that are felled to create wrappings and containers for your food products, or forests that are burned to clear space for the grazing of cattle, your beef supply? What of her blood (the petroleum waste in plastic) with which you fastidiously wrap and package every little bit and tiny morsel? And of the animals, the fish and other sea creatures that have been driven to extinction by your hunger? What of them? Do you think about the toxicity of your pesticides and growth hormones and all your artificial 'nutrients' ... and their effects on the soil, waters and air of Gaia?

As much as you sadden at the thought of no longer celebrating the sensual pleasures of food and all of the emotional gratification that it provides you, be reassured that all you really need for fuel is light. This has been shown to you throughout history by the Masters who have been able, through concentrated mind, to overcome the physical body's needs and simply survive by breathing light into the body electric. However, this practice for you is still the exception, whereas in the higher dimensions it is the rule.

As a superficial observation ... just think. If you have a poor relationship with food and are struggling to change your eating habits, you should be delighted to know that the struggle will soon be over!

Meanwhile, we have spoken of preparation, of awakening the light body, and have explained to you how every cell requires light. What you are now coming to understand is that the body needs only light to exist in higher dimensions. This is the aspect that may have eluded you, for it is difficult for you to comprehend living in light form. This is why many of your best teachers, the true gurus and guides, attempt to show you the significance of food and wean you away from the density of meat. And once again we ask you: how can you possibly evolve beyond your animal selves when you feed on animal blood and flesh?

Will you be physical in your movements, transporting yourselves into different environments? Here we enter into the difficult areas of our communications, for once again we must embark upon theories and considerations of the no-time, which is most difficult for you to perceive and even more complex in the telling. Nonetheless, know that if you can move to another event by resonating to the time of its occurrence, so can you travel to a destination by vibrating to its coordinates on the cosmic web.

We feel that you are not quite ready to unravel the mysteries inherent in the no-time paradigm, and so we will simply state that your current forms of transportation and the enormous waste that they produce will also disappear, as your evolution into the light body will no longer require mechanics and machines to take you where you wish to be. As you move out of 3D, you will be free to move around the planet by surfing the cosmic waves of the time-space continuum; so will you move through space and in and out of the higher and lower dimensions!

When you perceive beings in the ethers, energies or forms that seem to appear from nowhere, what is occurring is that a being or its thought form from another dimensional state or time has found resonance in your field, or in the vibrations held in a location, and has come to that frequency to experience its energy field. Perhaps, in the case of unresolved karma, it has returned to heal it. Those of you with heightened sensitivity usually perceive such beings as ghostly, transparent apparitions, but that is not a correct perception. What happens there is that the being who has surfed into a lower dimension, or more specifically a denser reality, cannot materialise at that level of compression. Therefore, you witness a sort of holographic representation of the entity's form, which fades in and out of your perception. It is similar to the experience of a television channel that isn't quite tuned in properly, where you see the images or hear the voice patterns fade into another programme and then fade out again.

This also applies to those who have managed to escape the grey zone, for we are not implying that everything beyond the physical is necessarily spiritually superior to your realm. Beings who are trapped in the grey zone are in distress, as they can neither evolve beyond the physical, nor re-enter it; they remain stuck in the illusion of non-existence and imprisoned in their unresolved karma. As you move over the zone in transfer, these entities attempt to connect, to attach to you in a sense — this occurs, unfortunately, more often than you can imagine. Many infants bring attachments through the birth canal with them, which explains why some beings are so troubled throughout the life experience. Some of those who are working through haunting memories of extraterrestrial abduction have most likely brought a grey or two through from birth. This explains why many who undergo hypnotic regression to deal with the terror of the experience uncover events involving alien visitation occurring from as far back as their early childhood.

The more you come to understand resonance, the more you realise how entities attach on various levels. You do draw to yourselves resonant thought forms, as they are manifest in the people who populate your immediate environment, as well as entities on the astral levels. There is no *wam*, no music in the grey zone; very little light or sound passes through the vaporous void, and yet thought waves which project out your lowest vibrations do penetrate its borders and into its deep inner fields.

You can understand why now, more than ever, you must clear your fields before moving through the astral chords of your Deity — for those of the grey zone do hope to 'cling on' and ride you into the light. Remember, when you send out negative thought waves it is as if you are throwing a lifeline into a morass of moving sands, for the trapped ones are capable of attaching to those thought forms and letting you literally pull them out of the quagmire.

Can you imagine, at a time when the entire solar system ascends, what that could mean to your new beginnings in the fourth dimension?

Fourteen

THE TRUE MEANING OF GENESIS

Y ou are developing a keen sense of understanding of the real values of numbers and their representation in energy forms and universal symbols. Yet, we believe that before you can conceptualise the Sirian perspective of sacred geometry and its appearance in the elemental patterns of the universe, you must master a fundamental understanding of number and archetypal form — since within them lie the building blocks of all creation. We have made repeated reference to these throughout these transmissions: the One; the two of duality and reflection; triangulation, the four points of the cross. Yet, the impact of such examples is only as profound as your understanding of the energies they reveal.

You are becoming more fascinated by the vibrational aspects of number now, as you heighten your conscious awareness of all that surrounds you and you are being activated to do so on many levels. This growing understanding of Sirian form and equation is reflected in the hyperdimensional geometry of your newly discovered 'fractal mathematics', which is moving you past the limitations of Euclidean planes and third-dimensional structure. It is in your awareness of the stars and their spatial dynamics, your computer-enhanced graphics of multidimensional constructs and your growing understanding of the galactic language of sacred geometry. We are projecting it onto your Earth plane in crop glyphs, hyperdimensional energy forms and, of course, through the instruments who are capable of bringing to the word the language of symbol and form.

The numerology of creation is simple, fundamental mathematics; sacred geometry replicates the explosion of life and all consciousness in the universe. It is so fundamentally simple that you may have overlooked the obvious, in your search to understand the greatness of Supreme Being and the universal design of intelligence. It is your past and future — the no-time, the All-That-Is — and we wish to remind you that within the symbols and oral traditions of human history, your architecture, music and art, lie the very configurations and geometric formulas that messengers such as ours are now transmitting from the 'higher dimensions'. Your believing, however, that we are the only source of the Wisdom not only dishonours you, but it creates once again an exoteric structure to which you look outside yourselves for the answers … and for empowerment. It limits your vision, for the Wisdom has always been available to you, laced throughout your experience: it is written in your great books; carved into the temple walls and painted in the caves. You will find it sculptured in the rocks and buried below the waters of your deepest oceans — your subconscious memories. It is the architecture of your very being. Most of you have just never deciphered the true meanings of your great works, nor searched to find or explore the hidden texts, for reasons we have discussed in other moments.

And so we, the Speakers of the High Council, are determined to stimulate your curiosity and challenge your preconceptions so that you reach the Source **directly** — straight arrow. We encourage you to examine the profound, unravel the mysteries and seek the truth, rather than to simply absorb our thoughts and adopt our visions. We wish to honour and celebrate you, assisting without intervening in your awakening. Ours is a desire to awaken you to your own greatness.

With that understanding, our statement of intent, we are now eager to expose to you the universal meanings — the Secret Wisdom — concealed in the Seven Days of Genesis, as recounted in the Old Testament of your Holy Bible. When you approach the material of your Bible with the intention of decoding it, you find clues to the origin of life embedded in the common language of its many translated texts. Meanings then change even more dramatically. Imposing Sirian consciousness of form and number into the holy scripts, a new interpretation surfaces. Many of the references that have been made throughout our writings find a new confirmation, validated through your enhanced understanding of their representation in form and number.

You may be surprised, even sceptical, to learn of the Secret Wisdom of numerology, form and equation as it is veiled in the traditional renderings of the Genesis passages. We know. We are walking on dangerous ground re-interpreting the Holy Book, for this is your religious heritage and you may feel you must defend the untouchable and sacred works. We ask that you trust our intention and join us for a most exquisite journey through the already well-known and trodden lands of interpretation, revealing to you the esoteric knowledge buried there, within the seven days of Genesis: the creation of the world.

The First Day

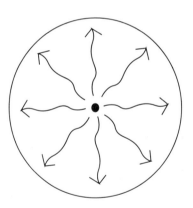

"In the beginning God created the heaven and the earth. And the earth was without form, and void; and darkness was upon the face of the deep. And the Spirit of God moved upon the face of the waters. And God said, 'Let there be light' and there was light. And God saw the light, that it was good ... And God called the light Day, and the darkness he called Night.
And the evening and the morning were the first day."

One is the number of Prime Creator. It is the initiator, the impulse, the primary vibration. Throughout your ancient writings,

hieroglyphics and the sacred rituals of indigenous peoples, the
two-dimensional representation of the universe appears consist-
ently as the circle, whose 'boundary' is equidistant to a central point
— the primary consciousness from which that very circle or universe has been created or defined. From the transcendent mandalas
of the Eastern religions, the Native Americans and other indigenous
peoples, to the sterile mechanics of the compass, the central point
is that necessary first experience of what can then be defined as
the circumference. It is the seed of expanding awareness, the
Godhead of radiating light.

Consider the specific elements of hidden or embedded meaning within this passage, the first day of Genesis, as they portray
the vibrational qualities of quantum physics, of number and of
form:

> 'In the beginning God created the heaven and the earth. And the
> earth was without form, and void; and darkness was upon the face of
> the deep.'

God (consciousness) is understood to create and permeate all
things, including the 'darkness', which you have long been taught
to fear and deny.

> 'And the Spirit of God moved upon the face of the waters.'

Consciousness, the creator of all realities, is depicted as moving
in waves — an expression of energy experienced in the oceans,
primarily upon the surface. Therefore, thought, the emanations of
consciousness, is understood to move in waves and this is a clue
to the quantum theory of vibrational mechanics.

> "And God said, 'Let there be light' and there was light. And God saw
> the light, that it was good … And God called the light Day, and the
> darkness he called Night."

Sound and light waves are introduced in this phrase. Since they
are 'pronounced' from God, they, too, are intended as emanations

of consciousness. Therefore, sound and light waves are projections of consciousness … the prime mover of all that which comprises the universe.

The Second Day

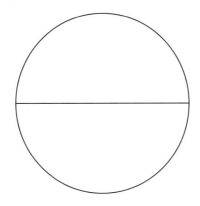

You are shown through the graphic elements of the circle how God can be depicted as consciousness radiating from the centre outward. If God, then, is envisioned throughout your religious history and the Secret Wisdom as 'male', it is attributed to the fact that such radiating force of movement is active, yang process. Take care not to confuse these energies with gender differentiations, for male and female are the absolute archetypes of all existence. You would do well to come to peace regarding that continuous war of the sexes that has marked your experience as human beings from the time of your seeding. Nowhere in the Secret Wisdom is 'male' considered superior to 'female', which appears with the division of the Godhead, or primary consciousness, into two.

> "And God said, 'Let there be a firmament in the midst of the waters, and let it divide the waters from the water.' And God made the firmament, and divided the waters which were under the firmament from the waters which were above the firmament: and it was so. And the evening and the morning were the second day."

Day two of Genesis describes the division of the whole, the separation of the All-That-Is into two equal halves; consciousness divided into complimentary aspects. From the moment of separation, the division of the whole, the poles of opposition seek to reunite and return to the One, and that is the dynamic tension inherent in all material reality. Here you are presented with reflection, the mirror and separation. Through subdivision, the fundamental building force of all existence, consciousness creates polarity: the attraction and repulsion essential to manifestation. It marks the electromagnetic dynamic; the symbol of male-female polarity.

The Third Day

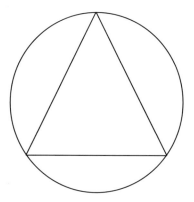

"And God said, 'Let the waters under the heaven be gathered together unto one place, and let the dry land appear.' And it was so. And God called the dry land Earth and the gathering together of the waters he called Seas: and God saw that it was good...
And the evening and the morning were the third day."

Day three of Genesis brings to the unfolding a third element: the 'dry land', so that now the aspects of existence are the 'heaven', the 'waters' and 'dry land'. You know this configuration in its geometrical representation, the triangle, which is the foundation of Euclidean geometry — for it is not until three elements appear that you perceive geometric form in that mathematical system. Composed of heaven, water and land, three appears throughout your spiritual teachings as the fundamental unit — the Holy Trinity. It is the father, mother and child; sperm, egg and foetus:

a most remarkable expression of the creative forces of the life experience. Most significantly, it is the aspect which emerges from polarity and then seeks to reconcile the separation of the whole.

Consider the recurrence of the Trinity in religion, art and human behavioural sciences and the impact of such a dynamic relationship. By investigating the patterns in the model, the 'set', you can relate the meaning of the third day to the archetypal triangle.

Once you have grasped the interrelatedness of those vibrations, the attraction of electricity (active consciousness) to its polar aspect, magnetism (subconscious receptivity), you will truly grasp the esoteric significance of the Trinity — the dynamics of interacting forces and the creative explosion of their union. 'Land' symbolises the crystallisation of that interaction into matter: it is form emerging ... it is the new life.

The Fourth Day

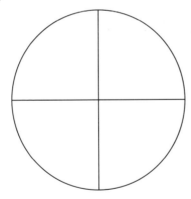

"And God said, 'Let there be lights in the firmament of the heaven to divide the day from the night, and let them be for signs, and for seasons, and for days, and for years, and let them be for lights in the firmament of the heaven to give light upon the earth.' And it was so. And God made two great lights; the greater light to rule the day, and the lesser light to rule the night: he made the stars also. And God set them in the firmament of the heaven to give light upon the earth. And to rule over the day and over the night, and to divide the light from the darkness: and God saw that it was good.
And the evening and the morning were the fourth day."

Day four of the Genesis myth provides a wealth of knowledge regarding the cyclical nature of life in physical reality, as portrayed by the birth of new form: the land. This text is rich in significance, as you are clearly aware, given the importance of the four vibration to all esoteric wisdom and your own experience as physical beings upon the Earth.

The cyclical nature of life on Earth is determined by the interdependence of the Sun and the Moon, described in the passage as the 'two great lights'. The Sun, the greater light, becomes the centre point around which Earth revolves; the Moon, the lesser light, orbits the Earth marking yet another universe. If we are to follow the earlier model of the point and the circle, God and the universe, we can deduce how the Sun became Earth's deity. The Moon, which orbits the Earth, marks yet another universe and her deity is Gaia, the Goddess. This is so throughout the heavens, just as it is reflected from the subatomic particles of your being through every cell and throughout your bodies.

The text describes the marking of days with the appearance of sunlight and moonlight, which rule day and night and which, combined, mark the time-frame of one day — Earth's complete rotation on its axis. The four seasons mark the Earth's complete rotation around the Sun: the cyclical measure of one calendar year.

Four adds volume to the mathematical form, bringing to Euclidean geometry the element of *depth*. From the simple two-dimensional triangle, you are now capable of constructing the three-dimensional form of the tetrahedron, which is identified in your science as the core structure upon which atoms, molecules and other life forms are built.

Four are the elements (air-fire-water-earth) upon the Earth; four the directions (of the horizontal plane); four seasons mark your rotation around the Sun and there are four phases of the Moon. Everywhere, the stability and order of the four vibration reflects to you the very nature of physical life on your planet and the primordial energies that constitute matter. So it is that by referring to the 'two lights' (the Sun and Moon), the fourth day of Genesis accounts for the forces behind the cyclical nature of life, the rhythms of Gaia, the patterns of generation and regeneration as aspects of the Sun and Moon — physical embodiments of the primordial subdivision of God-consciousness.

The Fifth Day

"And God said, 'Let the waters bring forth abundantly the moving creatures that hath life, and fowl that may fly above the earth in the open firmament of heaven.' And God created great whales, and every living creature that moveth, which the waters brought forth abundantly, after their kind, and every winged fowl after his kind. And God saw that it was good. And God blessed them saying, 'Be fruitful, and multiply, and fill the waters in the seas, and let fowl multiply on the earth.'
And the evening and the morning were the fifth day."

Five, the numerical representation of the pentagon and its inner pentagram (the five-pointed star), is the prevalent geometric form found in living beings, manifested in the bodies of most animals and human form. It represents the life force, the regenerative capacity of consciousness, which breathes life into the elements of composition within living things. You are being told how consciousness, the prime mover, activates the elements to create life. Again, it is the voice of God (the conscious will) that activates that process.

The Sixth Day

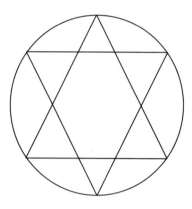

"And God said, 'Let us make man in our image, after our likeness: and let them have dominion over the fish of the sea, and over the fowl of the air, and over the cattle, and over all the earth, and over every creeping thing that creepeth upon the earth.' So God created man in his own image, in the image of God created he him; male and female created he them. And God blessed them, and God said unto them, 'Be fruitful, and multiply, and replenish the earth, and subdue it: and have dominion over the fish of the sea, and over the fowl of the air, and over every living thing which moveth upon the earth.' And God said, "Behold, I have given you every herb-bearing seed, which is upon the face of all the earth and every tree, in the which is the fruit of a tree-yielding seed; to you it shall be for meat. And to every beast of the earth, and to every fowl of the air, and to everything that creepeth upon the earth, wherein there is life, I have given every green herb for meat." And it was so. And God saw everything that he had made, and behold, it was very good.

And the evening and the morning were the sixth day.

Thus the heavens and the earth were finished, and all the host of them."

So many clues to the Wisdom are found in this, the recounting of the sixth day of Genesis, that an entire volume could be dedicated to it alone. In attempting to draw from the text the most salient clues, we invite you to contemplate the opening phrase:

"And God said, 'Let us make man in our image, after our likeness: and let them have dominion over the fish of the sea, and over the fowl of the air, and over the cattle, and over all the earth, and over every creeping thing that creepeth upon the earth.'"

Don't you find it odd that no one has ever addressed the contradictory usage of language in this godly statement, who refers to himself as 'us', and to man as 'them'? We suggest that the use of the plural pronouns in each case are the coded linguistic symbols which intend to trigger your understanding that all consciousness is thought waves which traverse the whole — and that the whole, the All-That-Is, recognises itself as an endless sea of infinite vibration and frequency.

You have long believed in a godly Father of human form because the term, 'in our image', has been misinterpreted from the first readings of the sacred texts. Across many cultures and throughout time, adepts of the Secret Wisdom have taught you the meaning of the axiom, 'As above, so below; and as below, so above', which is diagrammatically represented in the six-pointed star. We have shown you God as primal consciousness which radiates out from centre; we shall address that concept as the 'macrocosm'. We suggest that the microcosm, that spark of light that is your centre, also radiates throughout your being, which is every bit as much a universe as the macrocosmic whole — it is this reflection that is intended as being 'in God's image' in the words of the sacred text.

"So God created man in his own image, in the image of God created he him; male and female created he them."

Read beyond the obvious meaning: that God created men and women. The esoteric significance of this phrase is much more profound in scope and intent, for it describes the All-That-Is, the whole, as container of both elements of the yang and yin as is man (manifested consciousness). In the study of the Wisdom, you are guided to remove gender from your understanding of the terminology of 'male/female', and recognise it as the linguistic model of all polar opposites which comprise reality. Each human being, then, is a yang/yin, male/female, electromagnetic unit of consciousness.

> "And God said unto them, 'Be fruitful, and multiply, and replenish the earth, and subdue it: and have dominion over the fish of the sea, and over the fowl of the air, and over every living thing which moveth upon the earth.'"

Following the macrocosm/microcosm comparison of God to (wo)man, we suggest that the concept of replenishing the Earth is intended as the infusion of matter with the light of consciousness, to 'subdue it', and that one must illuminate the dense or lower self, if the human microcosm of the Godhead is to return to Source. It is the domination over the animal self which is the task that God (the macrocosm) asks of man (the microcosm).

The allusion to man's supremacy over the animal archetypes of the sea, air and earth (the 'waters, the heaven, and the dry land') is two-fold. First, that man's purpose as a co-creator is to rise above the animal self; and second, that by bringing light into the elements of matter at the cellular level, he achieves that purpose.

> "And God said, 'Behold, I have given you every herb-bearing seed, which is upon the face of all the earth and every tree, in the which is the fruit of a tree-yielding seed; to you it shall be for meat.'"

Here, in the sixth day of Genesis, you are gifted with the key to the accomplishment of that task, the awakening of the light body — the ascension from the density of matter (the 'earth' of the physical body) to light. In earlier teachings, we have shown you how that process requires the drawing of light into the cells of your bodies, for every cell is a universe within itself, a Godhead in its own right. So is the seed, the God-force and centre of the fruit, the radiating centre of its universe. Therein is hidden a great secret to the life force and creative fire that lies within the seed, and should offer you clarity as to its potency as food source.

> " ... to you it shall be for meat."

By now, after our numerous references to the importance of eliminating meat from your diets, we trust you understand that plant foods draw light into the cells, while animal meat increases the density and the darkness.

The Seventh Day

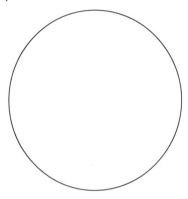

"And on the seventh day God ended his work which he had made: and he rested on the seventh day from all the work he had made. And God blessed the seventh day, and sanctified it: because that in it he had rested from all his work which God created and made."

The number seven defies definition and eludes form: a geometric oddity which does not follow the natural progression of the form and shapes which constitute the geometry of matter, as we have encountered them through the sixth. Yet, seven has long been honoured as the most mystical of all numbers, for it corresponds to the seven directions, the seven days, the seven chakras, the rays and endless other systems which inevitably reflect the ethereal aspect of the number. It is spectrum, prism and tone: levels, layers and aspects. Seven is the Sabbath day of rest and holy reflection … a most sacred numerological point of reference in many of your holy books and tradition. Is there a connection between that eccentricity, that elusiveness of form, and its mystical meanings?

Consider that the geometric seven, the heptagon, simply does not appear naturally in the world of dense matter. It is not present in the structure of the leaf, nor cell, crystal or dew drop. Yet, seven are the colours in the rainbow; the notes of the musical scale; the energy centres of the chakric system. Is this, the seventh day of rest, a symbol of consciousness manifesting its higher dimensionality … the 'dreamtime', perhaps, of God?

Day seven of Genesis describes God as 'resting from the work he had made'. The usage of the word, 'made', is deliberate, as it wishes to demarcate the work of conscious manifestation of matter which reaches completion in day six of the texts. Could it be that here, at day seven, you are being shown how God (consciousness) expresses 'his' diversity and immeasurable wisdom in the investigation of his own higher self? Seven does indeed belong to the realm of colour, music and spirituality, as it is the measure of the rainbow, the diatonic scale and the chakras — appearing as a reflection of the divine creativity which draws matter upward.

Like the gods of Olympus, lulled by the strumming of the seven strings of the Lyre, God rests by slowing his frequency. When he does, the visible spectrum (the rainbow) appears. Music, the harmonious reflection of sound, dances across the seven notes of the scale and through the universe echoes the Music of the Spheres. On the seventh day, God, the artist, lays the groundwork for your evolution out of matter — the chakra wheels of light, energy and vibration: divinity reaching for an ideal, the inspiration of the soul.

Do you recall the seventh direction? Imagine God going within — Prime Creator exploring 'himself' — and perhaps you will uncover the deeper meaning of the day of 'rest and blessings'.

Then will you understand the magic of the seventh day.

Fifteen

DNA AND THE GREAT EXPERIMENT

More and more information is being made available to you now, revealing how the biogeneticists of distant civilisations contributed to Gaia's development by depositing various DNA codes upon the planet through their seed — for what was to be the greatest experiment of the universe. You will need to weed through it all with much circumspection, in order to determine what you believe is credible and what feel like the ramblings of wild imagination. This you can achieve by listening to your gut response and inner guidance. You must do the same with *The Cosmos of Soul*, for not only do we welcome your scrutiny, we seek it from you. This is the true exchange; it is one of the ways that we reach each other.

Remember that the Wisdom is coded right into every sub-atomic particle of your being, just as it is in the leaf, a cloud and the very air you breathe. It is the collective intelligence, the Akasha, written in the ethers of All-That-Is. Know that you do access the Akasha all the time, particularly when you are centred and clear, and when your minds are uncluttered with the noise of logical deduction and analytical process.

We encourage you to hold that centre, the balance point, throughout our teachings and those of others who have come before and will come after. Accept what you feel is truth, or at least what you perceive as a possible reality, and discard whatever rings discordant in your hearts. Know, too, that what is true to you today will change quite dramatically in the days to come, bearing in mind that your openness to new thoughts and theorems paves the way to increased understanding and new vision. Despite the outward appearance of social decay and destruction, yours is a blessed generation. Therefore, be firm, but not rigid; discerning, but not sceptical. Above all, open your hearts with the clearing of your cluttered minds. This is the way of the Aquarian.

Since the beginning of this, your current calendar decade, Pleiadian Light Emissaries have also been intensifying their communication with you. The channels have been bringing through revolutionary teachings, which identify your true heritage: a far cry from the monkey business of missing links and Darwinistic platitudes. Your race is the brain child of many stellar beings, and like the Pleiadians, we took part in your very inception. We want you to know that, for we are your family as you are ours, and many are your distant relatives across the infinite expanse of the Cosmos.

You can understand why it is of such importance to us that you solve the DNA riddle and claim us as your ancestors. You are not the evolutionary brood of the gorilla; nor are you cousin to the chimpanzee, as you have been taught in the Darwinian context. You are a species unto your own, *Homo Sapiens*, seeded from many other systems and parallel galaxies ... star beings of the Earth Project.

As you were the hybrids of many species in the universe, your race was a multidimensional experiment in the extreme polar consciousness of physical reality. Originally, you were engineered with twelve strands of DNA, light codes of intelligence that would allow you all the gifts and potential of your stellar heritage — the genetic assemblage of some of the more evolved beings of the universe. You were designed to be the greatest of all intelligent life forms in the material universe, to master 3D like no other species had ever done before. In essence, we thought we could create a super race of light-bodied beings who would be capable of anchoring the higher frequencies, while crystallising form in the third dimension. That was our challenge. We believed it to be a light quest of noble intention.

Our Elders took part in the Earth Project, along with the Light Emissaries of many other dimensions and star systems. Never was there celebrated a greater victory than the seeding of Gaia — the successful genetic splicing of many species' DNA codes — which utilised a select strain of bacteria as the base structure into which snips of diverse genetic material were implanted, creating strands of what your scientists refer to as 'recombinant DNA'. Beings from many galaxies were united in that effort and your planet became, in many ways, the centre of the universe, as all eyes were upon you — the emerging super race of human beings. Earth energies vibrated golden across the Web, as expectation of the Great Race resounded through the Cosmos.

Gaia was to become the clearest light of the galaxy, the sweetest *wam* to play across the waves of the cosmic sea and the greatest communication station in the universe. The human being would be known as the golden child of creation: a flawless physical entity of supreme intelligence, Spirit and light.

There was another significance to the Earth Project, which we feel you have a right to know. You are most likely aware from your history, and that of your animals, that the genetic make-up of a species weakens with interbreeding. With time, defects in a genetically isolated species develop into weaknesses in the strain, which eventually dies out completely. This was an aspect of consideration in the seeding of Earth, for we believed that through the creation of the recombinant DNA, we were assuring the survival of many remote civilisations, which did not have access to other races with which to cross-breed. By creating the four master prototypes of the human race, each bearing genetic material of different species, we were assuring the survival of the genetic pool on Earth as well.

Soon after the gestation of these four master races, the polar forces of darkness moved in and took control of the planet in every sense of the word. You were left with only two active strands, the incomplete matrix, and that is how they have controlled you ever since. If they could have unplugged those as well, they would have, stripping you completely of all intelligence and the ancestral memory of your true origins. Fortunately, your existence depended upon the double helix, so they had no choice but to leave the two vital strands. The memory, you see, lies in those codes, for they form the nucleus of every single cell of your body and the controlling lords wanted you to forget forever the Family of Light.

This is why the core belief that yours is the only life in the universe was formed and implanted in your consciousness. It is why religions refuse to contemplate life on other planets, and why your governments hide their contact with beings of other worlds from the people of Earth. The antecedents of the power élite feared that, one day, you would be reactivated, and that day has finally arrived. Now is the time to remember.

Now is the time, dear ones, to remember.

We learned from the Experiment that, like your current genetic engineers, we were playing God to the extreme — overstepping our boundaries — and that such genetic tampering denied you the process of self-discovery and the journey of Spirit. It denied you the choice of which we have spoken with such emphasis and interfered with the Master Plan of the Creator. As infants of an evolving third-dimensional planet, you were never meant to hold that kind of super genetic wiring, for it was not harmonious with the very nature of evolution within your reality. Indeed, you were meant to populate Gaia in her physical stage of evolution and to awaken, as a race, along with her. It was meant to occur at this time, foreseen by Prime Creator, for your reaching the limits of physical reality and exacerbating the extremes of its polarity were all part of the very design of Gaia's evolution.

Do you comprehend the significance of what we are telling you here? We hope that you understand that the dark forces were allowed to disturb the process of your incubation because, like all other sentient species, you had to travel the road of soul ascension: no short cuts then, and none now.

Think back. Do you recall the thrill of diligently saving your money to buy your first used cars and the pride and sense of achievement that you derived from purchasing them yourselves? Surely you have remarked upon how much greater was your satisfaction than that of today's children, who demand your gifts of the flashy and new just out in the showrooms. Values, you see, are very much determined by your personal commitment, motivation and need. As free-will beings, you came in to create your own experience; make your own choices and know the focus of dedicating yourselves to an ideal. Quite simply, you came to do the work.

It was our intention to create a race of Super Gods on Earth. How could we have overlooked the obvious — that it is the spark of divinity within every life form that knows such title. It is the soul essence which creates the form and descends into matter and that is the creation of Prime Creator leaving itself; it is Divinity crystallising in matter to know the process of its return to the light. That is the purpose of the soul essence. No other architect but the Creator is capable of such design.

In our misguided enthusiasm, our ego-centred creativity, we believed a master race could be genetically constructed, forgetting that the very purpose of life is to become masters through the process of descending into the darkness and then returning to Source. Otherwise, there would be no reason to separate out as co-creators. Like Adam and Eve in paradise, everything would have been done for you. There would have been no motivation or reason for such a race of giants to exist at all.

We were humbled by the lesson of the Great Experiment, for Prime Creator allowed the darkness to destroy our masterpiece in order to teach us karmic debt, right action, and a fundamental understanding of the free will process. In a sense, we are just as responsible for your enslavement as are the lords of your subjugation. Having experienced divine intervention, we know now that it is against universal law to intervene in the karma of any sentient being. That is why you are misdirected if you believe that a Messiah is coming to save you, or that E.T.s will swoop down and free the Earth from the mad warriors, just as they are about to push the buttons of total destruction.

You must do it yourselves; it is all up to you now. We can offer you knowledge, support and insight — our love — but we cannot save you. What we can provide are the keys to the gateways, and that has been our mission in these teachings. But you are the ones who must turn them and walk through. Humanity simply cannot hole up in Fantasilandia any longer, pretending that you can just sit and gaze into the blur of your apathy and wait for things to magically resolve on their own. Once again, all eyes are upon you.

The universe is watching, waiting for you to take the evolutionary leap which moves you closer to the realisation of our vision, because (despite appearances) you are becoming that great race, just as Prime Creator had always intended. Now, as you are pulled ever closer into the vortex tunnel, you are being recoded with the additional strands as a natural extension of what had begun as an artificial experiment.

This is your legacy. You have earned it, for as evolving souls you have chosen to take part in the ascension of an entire solar family, the greater celestial body of your Solar Deity. Whatever personal experiences you have been focused upon until now, you will find yourselves shifting consciousness to a more galactic awareness of your purpose for reincarnating upon the Earth, as she moves into her fourth-dimensional body. Know that you are part of an élite group of beings, those fortunate ones who have directly participated in celestial ascension as residents of planets transmuting from the physical to the light body. These are amongst the rarest of events in the universe; they are exceptional moments in the all-time.

And you, the awakening, are part of it.

In conjunction with the transition of the Earth Mother, your personal evolutionary process allows now for the retrieval of a third strand of what the scientists refer to as 'junk DNA' — for you have evolved to it as awakening human beings of the twenty-first century. You understand the perfection of all life and its intricate form and manifestation, yet you accept the terms 'junk DNA' and 'grey matter' as biological truths and scientific reality. Do you really believe that, within your exquisite genetic make-up and complex neural networks, Prime Creator, the Great Architect, would have deposited waste?

Indeed, there is no junk or greyness within you. It is just that your scientists have yet to explain how the unidentified areas of the brain correspond to the disassembled strands of DNA. However, they are beginning to discover and recognise new connections as you are being recoded with the third strand, which plugs into your third energy centre, the power chakra. Given what we have told you of manipulation, is it any wonder that it was stripped from you?

Some are now being recoded with fourth, fifth, sixth and seventh strands, for the enlightened amongst you will be taking leaps into even higher dimensions than the fourth and that is your karmic reward. You have earned your wings. But for now, we wish to elaborate upon what is about to occur within most of you as the third strand of your DNA, a most crucial aspect of your evolving consciousness, is being reactivated.

Because, as Sirians, our understanding of all experience is founded upon the essentials of form and equation, we believe we can best explain the process in terms of mathematics and geometry. We ask that you let this be a point of departure from where you can now apply the theoretical dynamic of the Trinity, and the geometry of the triad, as we have defined them in the previous text. It will be important to your understanding of what is taking place in your accelerating light bodies that you meditate upon the diagrammatic form of its sacred geometry and internalise that numerical vibration.

If the essence of number is to be considered universal (and we do assure you that, as we understand it, patterns of number and form are a constant and universal reflection of the intelligence of creation), then in your current DNA model — two filaments swirling in mirror-imaging spirals — lies coded the polarity dynamic of duality, the incessant reflection of the yin/yang interaction. We are suggesting that polarity has actually been coded within you, right down to your genetic structuring. This is another explanation of how humanity has been entrapped within its extremes. You were taken down to two strands of DNA, held in the vibrations of survival and emotion and stripped of your true power, which is being activated now with the retrieval of the third strand. You are going to experience a quickening in your power centres like you never dreamed possible, despite the progress you have been making from your work on the energy body. We are talking about a Big Bang event taking place at the cellular level of your individual being, and then shining back out across the waves between you: a new light for humanity.

Understanding *three*, the creative explosion resulting from the electromagnetic attraction of the *two*, will give you a Sirian perspective of what is going to take place within and between you, once you have fully reintegrated the third helix. This is an essential key to the process of transformation, just before your solar system enters the preparatory phase of its passage through the astral chord of the Deity.

> With the activation of the third strand of DNA,
> you will experience the creative fire of
> one and two, male and female,
> electricity and magnetism
> as they 'connect'
> at the subatomic level.
> This is the trigger
> of your galactic rebirth.

Many have spoken of your rebirthing into the higher dimensions, as have we. You are ready now to understand what this means to your individual process, and how it is going to be accomplished at a genetic level within each human being who chooses to remain in body, as your entire system moves through the tunnel. Those who have not begun the process of clearing and who are still holding trapped energy and unresolved emotions, and those whose chakric systems simply are too stuck to anchor the light will not be taking part in the individual and planetary transmutation. Again, we remind you that that is a free-will decision which every sentient being on your planet will be required to make in these coming years of extraordinary change.

What exactly do we mean by 'individual transmutation'? As the third strand of DNA weaves its way into the existing double helix, it will knit together the other two strands, which currently coexist as complimentary, mirror patterns of each other. There, where the third strand unites these two, will the Son be born again. In essence, we are showing you that in your very make-up, your DNA treasure chest, you are experiencing the birth of a new form of consciousness. It is the triangulation of the light filaments of the universe, the Gossamer Web, that is now being woven within your inner galaxies. They, too, will reach across the waves and link up with the light beams of others whose DNA has so been altered.

Bearing in mind our teachings on number and form, ask yourselves what will occur in every single cell of your body as the third strand of DNA connects the double helix, forming triangulation. There will be an explosion of new form and new life within your cellular structures that will bring untold meaning to your concept of illumination. Can you imagine? We are talking here of one of the most significant moments in human development and you have chosen to be part of that great evolutionary leap into multi-dimensionality. Surely you are aware of the enormous significance of that choice.

The third strand of the dormant DNA, the so-called 'junk' within you, is being activated now, as the cosmic energies radiating through the atmosphere and into the body of Gaia intensify. Those of you who have done the conscious clearing will be the first to reach awareness of these altered vibrations. You will know by the intensification in your emotional bodies and your sense of heightened desire. You will be feeling energised, empowered and desirous of change — eager to take command of your lives in more productive ways. You will find yourselves clearing out the dead wood, exercising your free will over matters that at other times left you feeling helpless and misdirected, or worse: apathetic and passionless. It will be as if someone has lit a fire beneath you!

You recognise the awakening among you, for they are the free thinkers who are unafraid to stand against convention and speak of universal truths. They represent the new ethics of your Age, models of clarity of mind and Spirit, and they are making waves in the Dead Sea of Dogma — rocking the boat.

Is this you? Have you begun to reclaim your heritage: the light of absolute power burning inside you? If you have come to these teachings, you most surely are well into your transition, for ours is a message intended to touch those who have begun to lift the veil. As you let it down, the bright light of creation will shine incandescent in your souls and you will realise that you are over-coming the fear of all that once held you in darkness. What is power, after all, if not fearlessness?

The reorganisation of your DNA is the essence of your individual transmutation into light body, a process which can be accelerated by your conscious efforts to clear all toxicity of mind and emotion and heal your broken pieces. We have told you: the stakes are higher than ever now. The future is this moment, when you must set your intention and move swiftly towards your objectives.

Growing numbers of the awakening of Gaia are retrieving the fourth and fifth strands at this time, bringing to you information from the higher realms. And you are excited, for in your quick-ening you are dazzled by the frequencies and your sparkling insights. As individual units of consciousness, you have created the karma which determines how you will be evolving in this process and that will subsequently determine how well you assimilate the cosmic energies that are reactivating the dormant strands. There are even those of your realm who will be recoded with all twelve strands before the sacred passing. These are the Initiates who will serve the masses through the Desert Days, assisting those who will require support, while energetically joining the Earthkeepers in holding the planet's energy fields together.

Let there be no competition among you, for this is a personal experience and you are making the rules as you move through, setting your own pace. Now, more than ever, it is time you see in the other greatness unfolding, rather than reflections of 'who you are' or where you think you should be on the spiritual ladder. The unresolved ego will be a most formidable deterrent to your awakening. You must let go if you wish to anchor the light within you. You must let go of the ego self.

This is the preliminary to the ecstasy that awaits you, if you have not already begun to experience the activation of the third strand. Just imagine … the triangulation of light taking place within every nucleus of every cell of your body. Our words can only remotely describe the transformative power of what is about to occur within you, for such experience is beyond verbal expression. Indeed, it is beyond the conscious perception of the third dimension in which you have dwelled as a race since your inception upon the Earth. And yet, here you are … mutating into your light selves, about to integrate the brilliance of a light which has lain dormant within you for 100,000 Earth years. Does that give you a better perspective as to where you are in the scheme of things?

As you quicken to the new frequencies coming into your accelerating light bodies and the restructuring of your genetic grids, you will radiate as beacons for those who, like you, have begun the transmutational process. This is an aspect of your attraction to each other — your unification — which brightens the light of Gaia. As individual units, you will be anchoring the cosmic energies within you and then beaming them across the Web, furthering the process of the other. This is how it works, you see, the Gossamer Web of Light.

This is evolution in its purest sense, where everything is in a state of becoming — of returning to Source. It is the way of all self-aware beings, co-creators of the universe. We break away, diving fearlessly into the dark waters, to reinvent ourselves: to experience our uniqueness, a purpose, a dream. We confront ourselves as **One**, a Monad; we experience reflection, the **Two** of polarity; and then, moving ever upward, we explode with the inner light of **Three** — triangulation — birthing the new within us.

You are now at this point of the journey, a most remarkable moment on the ascending spiral upon which we are all moving closer to total integration in the splendour of the Infinite Light.

Acquirers of wisdom, we bring back to the All our individual experience of choice and unconditional love, from which more light emerges. We face the darkness, the 'devil', to learn the dynamics of fear and ignorance. We confront the 'enemy' to learn compassion and the power of forgiveness. We acquire ego consciousness as a means to understanding unity, the oneness of all things. With every lesson, we become lighter.

Always reaching for the light of love, we climb the mountains of adversity. Yes, there are moments when we slide into the deepest ravines, just as there are others … when we reach the peaks. We look down at where we've been, celebrating the arrival and then begin again, always moving towards higher ground … always striving for greatness. And to each, a different rhythm, a different pace and focus, for that is free will in motion.

All roads lead back home. That, dear ones, is the self-fulfilling prophecy of Supreme Being, the *All-That-Is, That-Has-Ever-Been* and *That-Always-Will-Be.*

EPILOGUE

Like the lotus, you experience three primary stages of evolution. The first is marked by ignorance and darkness, when you lie below the dense mud — a closed chrysalis — which, by nature of existence, will eventually be pulled upward by the warmth of the Sun. The second is exemplified by the climb through the clouded waters of your emotional experience, yet still the flower reaches to the Sun, knowing no other destiny … no other purpose. The third brings full illumination in the splendour of the light. The lotus flower blossoms, bearing its exquisite beauty to all those who are aware enough to recognise God unfolding.

You, the awakening, are reaching for the surface, about to open your petals in the warmth of the true light of existence. You are beautiful, majestic in your hearts and determined of will, and we celebrate you. Your clarity of intent lies within the seed, the pure consciousness that is all life. It is that which empowers you to reach beyond the obscurity of those murky waters; it is the vital force which drives all life to reach for the light.

Rock, tree, animal, human … you are all the crystalline reflection of the Divine Artist. Within every one of you is the spark of divinity which triggers the infinite unfolding of your many forms and dimensions, as you pass in and out of the tunnel of birth and rebirth upon your exquisite journey along the ascending spiral of Spirit.

Pioneers, you are the forerunners of the New World, a world you came to rediscover and transform together. This is the ultimate reunion, the greatest festival of life emerging … and we are with you. Children, we salute you. Yours is the task of reaching the light and then assisting the others and you will, for you are seekers of truth. Your hearts are opening, your minds alert and inquisitive, and the light of your souls is ever brighter. You are the emerging, the clear, shining faces, seeking that eternal radiance which has drawn you upward … higher and higher still, and we recognise you, lightworkers of Gaia. We know you.

There are many doorways … many openings, and you hold the keys. **You always have**. It is just that it has taken you until this point in your evolutionary journey to understand that they cannot hold you from your brothers and sisters of the galaxy any longer. The deception is coming to an end now, as you reclaim your stellar heritage and slowly begin to remember who you really are. There is a breathtaking universe for you to know, fantastic worlds of such incredible beauty and illumination that you will be stunned when you finally break free from the illusion of isolation and join the rest of the universe.

We have given you back that which is already yours — the keys to the universe. Use them as tools of self-discovery, and you will accelerate your passage. We will be there, welcoming you as you pass across the threshold, joining with beings from the far reaches of your imagination, other galaxies and dimensions. We long to embrace you, to show you our image without secrecy or limitation and to honour your journey, for you cannot imagine how far you will have travelled when you finally enter the portal and come through to the next dimension.

And as you walk through the winter of the Desert Days, remember to carry the lantern, so that the lost can find their way.

Our love surrounds you. Be fearless like the lion; acute as the eagle; and gentle like the dove: never doubting your strength; never losing your way; never forgetting that you are the

Gaian vibration rising.

THE SIXTH-DIMENSIONAL KEYS
TO THE UNIVERSE

As Above, So Below.
The blueprint of the macrocosm
is buried within the microcosm
and all is infinite.
From the seed the unfolding and from the leaf
regeneration.
Chapter Four

⤷

Every cell of your body is activated by Light.
Like a miniature battery, with north and south poles
Each cell holds within it the full rainbow spectrum ...
Food must be taken into the body to replenish
the light frequencies needed by the cellular
units of your body.
Chapter Six

⤷

The closing of the calendar
The end of time
will be a coming again to zero point...
your evolution out of the constraints
of third-dimensional reality.
Chapter Four

⤷

The brightest stars in your night skies
are so many millions of miles from Earth
that it takes years for their light to reach you…
Chapter Nine

↩

The devil is the fear you hold within you
The Luciferian aspect of your existence
Your chains, the darkness of ignorance
Are your prison.

Understanding death and passage
Birth and rebirth
Initiates the process of your emancipation
Your awakening…
Chapter Eleven

↩

Even the darkest beings
reflections of All-That-Is
Journey the spiral of ascension
eventually moving into the Light
for that is the nature of Spirit.
Chapter Twelve

↩

Only by integrating the
yin and the yang aspects of your own being
will the illusion of polarity of Spirit resolve.
When the Adam and Eve within you
become One
Then can you know and understand
the All-That-Is.
Chapter Thirteen

↩

With the activation of the third strand of DNA,
you will experience the creative fire of
one and two, male and female,
electricity and magnetism
as they 'connect'
at the subatomic level.
This is the trigger
of your galactic rebirth.

RECOMMENDED READING

Bailey, Alice, *Initiation Human And Solar*, Lucis Publishing Company.

Bates, Ernest, ed., *The Bible as Living Literature*, Simon & Shuster.

Bauvall, Robert and Gilbert, Adrian, *The Orion Mystery*, Reed International Books.

Briggs, John, *Fractals: The Patterns of Chaos*, Thames & Hudson.

Burr, Harold S., *Blueprint for Immortality*, C.W. Daniel Company Ltd.

Capra, Fritjof, *The Tao of Physics*, Shambala Books.

Friedman, Norman, *Bridging Science and Spirit*, Living Lake Books.

Frissell, Bob, *Nothing in This Book is True...* , Frog Ltd. Books.

Hancock, Graham, *Fingerprints of the Gods*, Crown Publishers.

Hesemann, Michael, *The Cosmic Connection*, Gateway.

Hoagland, Richard, The Mars/Moon Connection (video).

Hoagland, Richard, *The Monuments on Mars*, North Atlantic Books.

Hope, Murray, *The Sirius Connection*, Element Books.

Hunbatz Men, *Secrets of Mayan Science/Religion*, Bear & Company.

Icke, David, *The Robots' Rebellion*, Gateway.

Marciniak, Barbara, *Bringers of the Dawn*, Bear & Company.

Manning, Jeane and Begich, Nick, *Angels Don't Play This Harp*, Earthpulse Press.

Roberts, Jane, *The Nature of Personal Reality*, Bantam Books.

Rowan-Robinson, Michael, *Our Universe: An Armchair Guide*, W.H. Freeman.

Sauder, Richard, *Underground Bases and Tunnels*, Adventures Unlimited Press.
Schlemmer, Phyllis, *The Only Planet of Choice*, Gateway.
Sitchin, Zacharia, *When Time Began*, Avon Books.
Stevenson, Sandy, *The Awakener*, Gateway.
Von Franz, Marie-Louise, *Alchemy*, Inner City Books.
Weil, Andrew, *Spontaneous Healing*, Ballentine Books.
Wilson, Colin, *From Atlantis to the Sphinx*, Virgin Publishing.

INDEX

ABOUT THE AUTHOR

Patricia Cori has been clairvoyant all her life. In her healing work she focuses on releasing energy blocks and negative thought forms through crystals, as well as sound and colour healing. In 1995 she founded The Lightworks Association in Rome, as a healing centre, school and library. She offers workshops in Britain, Egypt, Thailand, the USA, Italy and Switzerland. She was raised in the San Francisco area and has lived in Italy since 1983. Patricia has been channelling the Speakers of the Sirian High Council since 1997.

For further information about her courses, seminars and workshops, please write to her care of:

Gill & Macmillan Publishers
Hume Avenue
Park West
Dublin 12

or to her e-mail address:

<patcori@tiscalinet.it>